TenThings
Every Child
with Autism
Wishes You
Knew

UPDATED & EXPANDED EDITION

TenThings

Every Child with Autism Wishes You Knew

Ellen
Notbohm

FUTURE HORIZONS INC.

Ten Things
Every Child with Autism Wishes You Knew
All marketing and publishing rights guaranteed to
and reserved by

FUTURE HORIZONS INC.

721 W. Abram Street
Arlington, TX 76013
800-489-0727
817-277-0727
817-277-2270 Fax
Website: www.FHautism.com
E-mail: info@FHautism.com

© 2012 Ellen Notbohm
Website: www.ellennotbohm.com
Email: emailme@ellennotbohm.com
Facebook: https://www.facebook.com/ellennotbohm (Ellen Notbohm, Author)
Twitter: EllenNotbohm
LinkedIn: Ellen Notbohm

For foreign rights inquires, please contact the author at emailme@ellennotbohm.com.

ISBN: 9781935274650

Publisher's Cataloging-In-Publication Data
(Prepared by The Donohue Group, Inc.)

Notbohm, Ellen.
  Ten things every child with autism wishes you knew / Ellen Notbohm. -- Updated & expanded ed.

  p. ; cm.

  Originally published: 2005.
  Includes index.
  ISBN: 978-1-935274-65-0

  1. Autism in children. 2. Autistic children--Care. 3. Autistic children--Family relationships. 4. Child rearing. I. Title. II. Title: 10 things every child with autism wishes you knew

RJ506.A9 N68 2012
618.92/85882

Printed in the United States of America

Praise for *Ten Things Every Child with Autism Wishes You Knew*

"The FIRST book you should read when your child is diagnosed. Written by a mum with fantastic insight into the world of autism, through the child's eyes, and having a son of her own with ASD really shines through in the book. It is an intelligent and empathetic book written FOR our children. Ellen Notbohm is an amazing mother and author! Have bought this book for ALL my family."

—Trinny Holman

"This book has become my Bible! Was like someone had switched on a light after reading it! Brilliant!!"

—Becky Gillingham

"This book is the only one that explained my son 100%. Nobody, not even medical doctors, were able to explain to me what my son is feeling. I often used to say, 'I wish I could see through his eyes for just one day.' This book made that possible."

—Caroline Nel

"After reading many autism books, this was the one for me. I laughed and cried my way through it. It gave me a sense of peace and relief to know I wasn't the only one who understood what was going on. It gave me relevant strategies and brought new concepts that were actually helpful. This book was about my son and I loved how positive it was!"

—Karen Maher

"(Ellen) and Bryce are my heroes, and changed my life in ways I can't describe, (as) *Ten Things* changed our family."

—Debi McCombs Garrett

"This was the first and only autism book I read after diagnosis. Positive and inspirational, it made me think about it from my son's view and not a parent's point of view. With every struggle or change or thought, I now always try to see it from his view and this enables me to think about how to help him in a different way."

—Claire Coley

"Absolutely *Ten Things* changed the way I looked at my son's behavior. Having it written from the child's point of view that really resonated with me and my husband—the parts about sensory issues and how not to use metaphors when speaking. That was huge for us. I bought several copies and gave it to teachers as well. Whenever I'm asked for book recommendations explaining autism, it's the first book I suggest."

—Kay Thomas

"I recently used [a summary of *Ten Things*] as a supplement to an autism presentation I gave to firefighter/paramedics. It was a HUGE hit! Prior to this, I made my family members read it as well. What great insight for them to have! Thank you again."

—Ray Di Lisi

"I love this book, and made it available to [my son's] school team as well. For us, it reiterated and clarified that our son does the absolute best every day to manage his world, and that we need to acknowledge and be proactive in providing him the best possibilities in his day."

—Lisa Todnem

"It is as important as the Declaration on Human Rights in France in 1789, no less."

—Jean-louis Jaucot

"Your book *Ten Things Every Child with Autism Wishes You Knew* is both my four-year-old son's and my own favorite book at the moment. For me, it's the insight and that it's everything I've ever wanted to tell the people around us, but did not have the words for. For him, it's the fingers on the cover. We both thank you."

—Siw Waag Halsen

Also by Ellen Notbohm

*1001 Great Ideas for Teaching and Raising Children
with Autism or Asperger's*

with co-author Veronica Zysk

Silver Medal, Independent Book Publishers Awards

Learning magazine's Teacher's Choice Award

Ten Things Your Student with Autism Wishes You Knew

with Veronica Zysk

Finalist, ForeWord Book of the Year Awards

iParenting Media Award

onlinecolleges.net's The 20 Essential Books About Special Education

The Autism Trail Guide: Postcards from the Road Less Traveled

Finalist, ForeWord Book of the Year Awards

Finalist, Eric Hoffer Book Awards

For Connor and Bryce

because they are doing such a good job of raising me

Contents

Preface

When *Children's Voice* published my article "Ten Things Every Child with Autism Wishes You Knew" in 2004, I could scarcely have anticipated the response. Reader after reader wrote to tell me that the piece should be required reading for all social-service workers, teachers, therapists, and relatives of children with autism. "Just what my daughter would say if she could," said one mother. "Screams wisdom throughout every word and sentence," said another. The article traveled from website to website, around the world: United States, Canada, France, Denmark, Hungary, Croatia. Iceland, Thailand, Poland, The Netherlands. Brazil, Venezuela. Australia, New Zealand, South Africa. Turkey, Morocco, Dubai, Iran, Singapore, South Korea, Taiwan, Japan. The sheer volume of interest and the diversity of the groups who found it relevant humbled me. They included hundreds of autism and Asperger's groups, but also support groups for chronic pain, obesity, assistance dogs, inner ear disorders, homeschoolers, religious school educators, knitting circles, food retailers. "I have a strong sense that your message crosses over to many special needs," wrote a social worker in the Midwest.

"Ten Things" quickly took on a life of its own; why exactly was it resonating so loudly? I decided that the resonance came from the fact that the piece spoke with a child's voice, a voice largely unheard in the rising uproar about autism. The continuing, often-tumultuous dialogue is productive and welcome. But what could be more ironic than that the subjects of the discussion are widely exemplified by the inability to express and advocate for themselves? I had seen several articles that took related approaches: ten things teachers want parents to know, or what mothers wish their children's teachers knew, what dads of children with autism need to know. When my editor, Veronica Zysk, presented me with one such adult-to-adult piece, I asked myself, who speaks for the child?

You do, came the self-reply.

"Write the piece," Veronica urged.

My grandmother liked to say that when you talk to yourself, you always get the answer you want. *Who speaks for the child?* I felt fortunate that my son Bryce's voice had been heard, thanks to committed teamwork among family members, school staff, and community resource workers. I ardently wanted his level of success to be the norm, not the exception. The original article, and later, this book, flowed from that.

Individual and collective attitudes about autism form under the influence of the language we choose in defining it. The incendiary and provocative remarks and opinions, whether intentional or thoughtless, commandeer our attention. We may respond to them, we may despair of them. But it may be the squadron of subtleties and nuances of language flying under our radar that does more to impede the development of healthy outlooks about a child's autism. Throughout the book, you will be asked to contemplate how the language of autism shapes your perspective. It will help you view autism from angles you may not have yet considered. There are also a few things you won't see.

You won't see autism referred to as a disability or a disease, unless I am quoting others or sources.

You won't see the word "disorder," except where it applies to other conditions as part of a name, as in attention deficit/hyperactivity disorder (ADHD).

I no longer use the term "neurotypical" to describe persons who don't have autism.

You won't see the word "autism" capitalized in this book unless it's at the beginning of a sentence or part of a name or title. We don't capitalize breast cancer, diabetes, glaucoma, anorexia, depression, or other conditions that don't include someone's name, like Asperger's. Capitalizing "autism" makes a visual statement that assigns it an authority and power it doesn't deserve.

And finally, the word "normal" never appears in this book outside quotation marks. The early days following our son's diagnosis of autism were spiked with questions from others along the lines of "Do you think he'll ever learn to be normal?" I found these questions at first stupefying, and later, presumptuous in a manner that almost made me pity the asker. I learned to answer the question with a smile and a wink and "When there comes a time that there is such a thing" or

"If he does, he'll be ahead of me." Then and now, I quoted Canadian songwriter Bruce Cockburn, who put it, "the trouble with normal is it always gets worse."

"A Word about Normal" is my favorite passage from my book *1001 Great Ideas for Teaching and Raising Children with Autism and Asperger's*. In it, a middle school speech therapist answers a mother's concern that her son hasn't made many friends and might not "do all the normal teen things we did."

> "When your son came to me last year," the speech therapist tells Mom, "his social thinking skills were almost nonexistent. He didn't understand why he should say hi to people in the halls, he didn't know how to ask a question to further a conversation, or how to engage with a peer during the lunch hour. Now he's working on those things. That's a huge amount of progress."
>
> "But he's only made two friends."
>
> "I would rephrase that: he's made two friends! One shares his interest in model trains and one shares his interest in running. He knows how you feel, though. So I am going to share with you what he told me the other day. He said, 'I don't want a lot of friends. I can't handle a lot of friends. More than one at a time stresses me out. I can talk to these two friends about things I'm interested in. They are great for me.'
>
> "Walk through this or any other school," the SLP continues. "You'll see a huge range of 'normal' middle school behavior.

You'll see nerdy normal, sporty normal, musical normal, artsy normal, techie normal. Kids tend to gravitate to groups that make them feel safe. For now, your son has found his group. You and I walk a fine line: honoring his choices while continuing to teach him the skills he needs to feel comfortable expanding his boundaries."

Your child has many social selves. To embrace all of them, and therefore him as a whole child, is to redefine how we view "normal"—one person at a time.

Although the Ten Things presented in this book characterized my child, they won't and can't possibly apply in total to all children with autism. Rather, you will see some of the characteristics and needs in every child with autism in degrees that vary from child to child, and from hour to hour, day to day, and year to year in an individual child. With education, therapy, and maturity—yours included—the limitations imposed by some of these characteristics may diminish, and some of those so-called limitations may be re-channeled in such a manner that you come to see them as strengths. When you reach the end of this book and in the days that follow, you may find yourself in a new and more interesting place on your child's autism spectrum than where you started. I hope so.

So, why a second edition of *Ten Things Every Child with Autism Wishes You Knew* when millions have read the first edition and its appeal remains strong? Why fix something that isn't broken?

In his book and film *Journey of the Universe,* evolutionary philosopher Brian Thomas Swimme describes the Milky Way galaxy "not as a thing, but as an ongoing activity." Such is the autism spectrum, an ever-exchanging sphere of being within a larger universe. We travel the continuum, sometimes hurtling along, sometimes stalling out, but each particle—child, parent, teacher, sibling, grandparent, friend, stranger—has his or her own place in the (sometimes elusive) order of things. That spot on the spectrum shifts over time. Experience and maturity change our perspective. The years that have passed since I wrote *Ten Things* encompassed my sons' teen years and transitions to adulthood. How could that not have altered my position on the spectrum? Those years also saw a global increase in autism that baffles and alarms everyone with a pulse (everyone but the cult-level cynics). My place on the spectrum shifted in the face of my own experiences, but also in response to the experiences of others who came into my life because of *Ten Things*. Some of my original thinking has morphed into larger thought. Some of it no longer seems relevant. Autism is as complex as it ever was, and the rising number of children with autism among us demands attention even from those who would rather turn their conscience and public dollars away. We defend and advocate for our children with more eyes upon us than we did just a decade ago. By conscription, we have become not just advocates, but emissaries. Being an autism parent today requires not only stamina, curiosity, creativity, patience, resilience, and diplomacy—but the courage to think expansively and to dream accordingly.

Thus, a second edition of *Ten Things*, faithful to its core being but, as I have myself, ripened with time—expanded and expansive.

Who speaks for the child? It does require a level of presumption to think that any one of us can get inside someone else's head and speak for them. I hope I can be forgiven for this, in the light of the overwhelming need to understand the world as the child with autism experiences it. It falls on us to grant legitimacy and worth to their different way of thinking, communicating, and navigating the world. It demands that we give voice to their thoughts and feelings, even when their voices are nonverbal. If we don't, the legacy of our children's autism will be opportunities untouched, gifts forever undiscovered. They are our call to action.

It begins ...

As the mother of a young child with autism, I quickly learned that on some days, the only predictable thing was the unpredictability; the only consistent attribute—the inconsistency. Much about autism baffles us, even those who spend their lives around it. The child who lives with autism may look "normal," but his behavior can be perplexing and downright unruly.

Not so very long ago, professionals thought autism to be an "incurable disorder." The notion of autism as an intractable condition with which no person can live meaningfully and productively has crumbled in the face of knowledge and understanding that continue to increase even as you read this. Every day, individuals with autism show us that they can overcome, compensate for, and otherwise manage many of autism's most challenging aspects as part of their fulfilling and dynamic lives. Many who live with autism not only do not seek a "cure," but reject the concept. In a widely read *New York Times* article in December 2004, Jack Thomas, a tenth grader with Asperger's syndrome, got the world's attention by stating, "We don't have a disease, so we can't be cured. This is just the way we are."

Jack and I are on the same page. When people who don't have autism frame its challenges only through the lens of their own experiences, they unwittingly close the door to the kind of alternative thinking that will make or break how far those with autism or Asperger's can go.

Perspective is everything. When I speak to parent groups, I ask them to jot down brief descriptions of their children's most challenging behaviors, and then to rephrase them in the positive. Is the child standoffish, or able to entertain herself and work independently? Is she reckless, or adventuresome and willing to try new experiences? Is she obsessively neat, or does she have outstanding organizational skills? Does she pester you with endless questions, or does she have a curiosity about her world as well as tenacity and persistence? Why do we try to fix the kid who perseverates but admire the one who perseveres? Both are forms of the same word meaning "refuses to stop."

Here's the one I hate the most: Does your child "suffer from autism," or does he live with autism?

Choose life over suffering.

For five years, I wrote a column for *Autism Asperger's Digest* called "Postcards from the Road Less Traveled." My editor, Veronica Zysk, and I thought the connection to Robert Frost's poem apt.

Two roads diverged in a wood, and I—
I took the one less traveled by,
And that has made all the difference.

A reader disagreed. "Postcards are from people who are having a good time on a trip," he wrote. "I'm not sure if that's what you want to portray."

I think postcards are more than that. They let loved ones know you've arrived at a certain place safely. They say, "I am thinking of you though I am far away," and they share the sights so they can be with you across the distance. They may recount trip-related woes and how they resolved them, sometimes with a bit of humor.

So my answer to that reader was yes, that is exactly what I want to portray, in my columns, in this book, and in my dialogue with parents, professionals, and the rest of the word. I am having a good time on this trip. The trip has been fueled by hope, possibility, undreamed-of accomplishments (my son's, mine and my whole family's), and ROI, return on investment.

But we did not start out from there.

We started with a basically sweet-tempered but nonverbal child who would lapse into bewildering episodes of hair-tearing, cat-scratching, furniture-throwing violence. He physically backed away from many classroom and playtime activities with his hands over his ears; he laughed at all the wrong times. He wore clothes only when socially necessary and didn't seem to experience pain or cold in a typical way.

A public school early intervention team identified Bryce's autism at age three. I went through the five stages of grief in the time it took to end the initial meeting. My older son Connor had been identified two years earlier with attention deficit/hyperactivity disorder (ADHD). I already knew about the therapies, the social challenges, the never-ending vigilance—and the exhaustion.

Raw fear motivated me. I could not bear to imagine Bryce's fate as an adult if I did not do everything within my power to equip him to live in a world where I would not always be around. I could not rid my head of words like "prison" and "homeless." Not for a nanosecond did it occur to me to leave his future to the professionals or to the ephemeral idea that he might outgrow his autism. His quality of life was at stake, and failure was not an option. These thoughts propelled me out of bed every morning and drove me to take the actions I did.

Jump a few years ahead with me now to the turn of the twenty-first century. At the school assembly, adorable first graders step to the microphone one after another to answer the question, "What do you want to be in the new millennium?" A soccer star! is a popular response. A pop singer! A race car driver! Cartoon artist, veterinarian, firefighter!

Bryce has considered the question carefully.

"I think I'd just like to be a grown-up."

Applause breaks out and the principal speaks deliberately. "The world would be a better place," he says, "if more people aspired to what Bryce aspires to."

Here is the gist of what I know to be true. Your child's autism does not mean that he, you, and your family will not lead full, joyous, meaningful lives. You may be scared, but dare to believe this, with a caveat. How much of that full measure we achieve with our kids depends upon the choices we make for and about them given their individuality and uncommon character. A memorable passage from Nora Ephron's story *Heartburn* has the protagonist, Rachel Samstat, asserting that when your "dream breaks into a million tiny little pieces, it leaves you with a choice. You can either stick with it, which is unbearable, or you can go off and dream another dream."

If you're reading this as a newcomer to the world of autism, I say, autism itself is not awful. Not understanding it, not having people around you who understand it, not getting the help that is out there for your child—that can be very awful. You're at the beginning of your journey, and we won't deny that it's a long one. And you would not undertake any long journey without first learning a little about your route. This book will alert you to signposts you will likely pass along the way, so that when you do, they will have a familiar look to them and be less foreign and frightening.

Some of you are already acquainted with the challenges of autism, sport a few scars too, I'll bet. This book can speak for you and your child to those who need to hear your message: teachers, parents, siblings, in-laws, babysitters, coaches, bus drivers, peer parents, friends of siblings, clergy, neighbors. Pass it around. Watch the barriers fall.

This book will equip those around our children with basic understanding of autism's primary elements. That understanding has a tremendous impact on the children's ability to progress toward productive, independent adulthood. Autism is complex, but throughout my experience, I've seen its myriad characteristics fall into four fundamental areas: sensory processing challenges, communication delays and impairments, elusive social thinking and interaction skills, and whole child/self-esteem issues. All are crucial. Here's why:

Sensory processing challenges. It's inescapable. A child cannot be expected to absorb cognitive or social learning, or "behave," when he experiences his environment as a constant bombardment of unpleasant sensations and nasty surprises. Your brain filters thousands of multiple-sensory inputs (what you see, what you hear, what you smell, etc.) simultaneously. His does not. It can provoke the equivalent of twenty-four-hour road rage as all those signals jam hopelessly in the brain stem. Think of how you feel trapped in the stifling fumes and racket of stalled traffic with no ability to affect your situation.

Communication delays and impairments. Without adequate means of expression, needs and wants remain unmet. The inevitable result is anger and frustration, not learning and growing. The ability to communicate, whether through spoken language, pictures, signing/semaphore or assistive technology, is bedrock.

Social thinking and interaction skills. Elusive and ephemeral, these skills differ from culture to culture, from setting to setting within a culture, and from relationship to relationship. Inadequacy or lack of them can isolate a child to a devastating degree. The child with autism, who truly doesn't "get it," paddles against a brutal current in first comprehending, then executing.

Whole child/self-esteem issues. Every last person on the planet is a package deal. We want to be accepted and appreciated for who we are as a whole, not a bundle of traits and quirks to be cherry-picked at will by others. The child with autism does need skilled guidance to achieve a comfortable place in the larger world. Working toward that goal with positive energy and optimism does not constitute fixing the child. They already possess much that can be celebrated; we must now go out and love and guide them with the same acceptance of whole self we want for ourselves.

Bryce's successes spring from that solid sense of self-esteem, his hard-won comfort with his physical environment and his ever-expanding ability to express himself. With those pieces in place, social and cognitive learning followed. As his life became easier, so did mine. Each passing year brought deeply gratifying feats: the day he swam to a trophy finish in a citywide swim meet, the day he sang and danced his way through *Charlie and the Chocolate Factory* as Grandpa Joe. The day he rode his two-wheeler for the first time, the time we worried no one would come to his birthday party and forty people showed up. His elation at making it through his first Scout campout, and his utter euphoria after successfully working up the nerve to ask the girl he'd admired since kindergarten to dance at the sock hop, and years later, to be his date for the prom. Running, running through six years on the middle school and high school track teams. Brandishing his first paycheck.

In time I came to realize that I would not change him even if I could. I wouldn't take his autism away. Wouldn't want to have missed any of the odyssey that made him what he is today.

Though the four elements we've just discussed may be common to many children with autism, keep in mind that the reason we call it a spectrum is that no two (or ten or twenty) children with autism will be completely alike. Each will be at a different point on that spectrum. And, just as importantly, every parent, teacher, and caregiver will be at a unique point in their understanding of the spectrum. Like the millions of pixels that comprise a television image, each person involved is a complicated composite. That's why there is no single recipe for success, no substitute for the research, self-education, and legwork necessary, and little window for complacency. Guiding, educating and appreciating the child with autism will be a continual work-in-progress. The revered opera diva Beverly Sills, mother of two special needs children, once said, "There is no shortcut to anyplace worth going." True, but the journey can be steeped in the joy of discovery. The guidebook is in your hands. Let's get started.

Here are ten things every child with autism wishes you knew.

I am a child.

My autism is part of who I am, not all of who I am. Are you just one thing, or are you a person with thoughts, feelings, preferences, ideas, talents, and dreams? Are you fat (overweight), myopic (wear glasses) or klutzy (uncoordinated)? Those may be things that I see first when I meet you, but you're more than just that, aren't you?

As an adult, you have control over how you define yourself. If you want to single out one characteristic, you can make that known. As a child, I am still unfolding. Neither you nor I yet know what I may be capable of. If you think of me as just one thing, you run the danger of setting up an expectation that may be too low. And if I get a sense that you don't think I "can do it," my natural response will be, why try?

My senses are out of sync.

This means that ordinary sights, sounds, smells, tastes, and touches that you may not even notice can be downright painful for me. My environment often feels hostile. I may appear withdrawn or belligerent or mean to you, but I'm just trying to defend myself. Here's why a simple trip to the grocery store may be agonizing for me.

My hearing may be hyperacute. Dozens of people jabber at once. The loudspeaker booms today's special. Music blares from the sound system. Registers beep and cough, a coffee grinder chugs. The meat cutter screeches, babies wail, carts creak, the fluorescent lighting hums. My brain can't filter all the input and I'm in overload!

My sense of smell may be highly sensitive. The fish at the meat counter isn't quite fresh, the guy standing next to us hasn't showered today, the deli is handing out sausage samples, the baby in line ahead of us has a poopy diaper, they're mopping up pickles on aisle three with ammonia. I feel like throwing up.

And there's so much hitting my eyes! The fluorescent light is not only too bright, it flickers. The space seems to be moving; the pulsating light bounces off everything and distorts what I am seeing. There are too many items for me to be able to focus (my brain may compensate with tunnel vision), swirling fans on the ceiling, so many bodies in constant motion. All this affects how I feel just standing there, and now I can't even tell where my body is in space.

Distinguish between won't (I choose not to) and can't (I am not able to).

It isn't that I don't listen to instructions. It's that I can't understand you. When you call to me from across the room, I hear "*&^%$#@, Jordan. #$%^*&^%$&*." Instead, come over to me, get my attention, and speak in plain words: "Jordan, put your book in your desk. It's time to go to lunch." This tells me what you want me to do and what is going to happen next. Now it's much easier for me to comply.

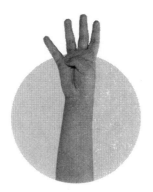

I'm a concrete thinker.
I interpret language literally.

You confuse me by saying, "Hold your horses, cowboy!" when what you mean is, "Stop running." Don't tell me something is "a piece of cake" when there's no dessert in sight and what you mean is, "This will be easy for you to do." When you say, "It's pouring cats and dogs," I see pets coming out of a pitcher. Tell me, "It's raining hard."

Idioms, puns, nuances, inferences, metaphors, allusions, and sarcasm are lost on me.

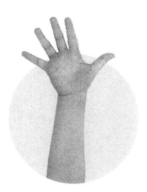

Listen to all the ways
I'm trying to communicate.

It's hard for me to tell you what I need when I don't have a way to describe my feelings. I may be hungry, frustrated, frightened, or confused but right now I can't find those words. Be alert for body language, withdrawal, agitation or other signs that tell you something is wrong. They're there.

Or, you may hear me compensate for not having all the words I need by sounding like a little professor or movie star, rattling off words or whole scripts well beyond my developmental age. I've memorized these messages from the world around me because I know I am expected to speak when spoken to. They may come from books, television, or the speech of other people. Grown-ups call it echolalia. I may not understand the context or the terminology I'm using. I just know that it gets me off the hook for coming up with a reply.

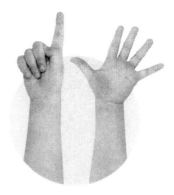

Picture this!
I'm visually oriented.

Show me how to do something rather than just telling me. And be prepared to show me many times. Lots of patient practice helps me learn.

Visual supports help me move through my day. They relieve me of the stress of having to remember what comes next, make for smooth transition between activities, and help me manage my time and meet your expectations.

I need to see something to learn it, because spoken words are like steam to me; they evaporate in an instant, before I have a chance to make sense of them. I don't have instant-processing skills. Instructions and information presented to me visually can stay in front of me for as long as I need, and will be just the same when I come back to them later. Without this, I live the constant frustration of knowing that I'm missing big blocks of information and expectations, and am helpless to do anything about it.

Focus and build on what I can do rather than what I can't do.

Like any person, I can't learn in an environment where I'm constantly made to feel that I'm not good enough and that I need fixing. I avoid trying anything new when I'm sure all I'll get is criticism, no matter how "constructive" you think you're being. Look for my strengths and you will find them. There is more than one right way to do most things.

Help me with social interactions.

It may look like I don't want to play with the other kids on the playground, but it may be that I simply do not know how to start a conversation or join their play. Teach me how to play with others. Encourage other children to invite me to play along. I might be delighted to be included.

I do best in structured play activities that have a clear beginning and end. I don't know how to read facial expressions, body language, or the emotions of others. Coach me. If I laugh when Emily falls off the slide, it's not that I think it's funny. It's that I don't know what to say. Talk to me about Emily's feelings and teach me to ask, "Are you okay?"

Identify what triggers my meltdowns.

Meltdowns and blow-ups are more horrid for me than they are for you. They occur because one or more of my senses has gone into overload, or because I've been pushed past the limit of my social abilities. If you can figure out why my meltdowns occur, they can be prevented. Keep a log noting times, settings, people, and activities. A pattern may emerge.

Remember that everything I do is a form of communication. It tells you, when my words cannot, how I'm reacting to what is happening around me.

My behavior may have a physical cause. Food allergies and sensitivities, sleep problems and gastrointestinal problems can all affect my behavior. Look for signs, because I may not be able to tell you about these things.

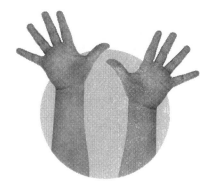

Love me unconditionally.

Throw away thoughts like, "If you would just—," and "Why can't you—?" You didn't fulfill every expectation your parents had for you and you wouldn't like being constantly reminded of it. I didn't choose to have autism. Remember that it's happening to me, not you. Without your support, my chances of growing up to be success¬ful and independent are slim. With your support and guidance, the possibilities are broader than you might think.

Three words we both need to live by: Patience. Patience. Patience.

View my autism as a different ability rather than a disability. Look past what you may see as limitations and see my strengths. I may not be good at eye contact or conver-sation, but have you noticed that I don't lie, cheat at games, or pass judgment on other people?

I rely on you. All that I might become won't happen without you as my foundation. Be my advocate, be my guide, love me for who I am, and we'll see how far I can go.

Chapter One

I am a whole child.

"Are you familiar with the term 'autism'?"

That question from Bryce's early childhood special education teacher marked the first time I heard the word autism applied to my child. For me, as for many parents, it was a scary moment, because that one word scrambled my image of my child's future and tossed it into unsurveyed terrain. Perhaps the most penetrating dread known to humans is fear of the unknown, a fear so fearsome it eludes a phobia designation. But in that first daunting moment, the October sun pierced the wall of windows behind me and settled like a reassuring hand on my back. Against the dark monolith of all I didn't know about autism, one luminous thing I did know shone through: my son was the same child I had fallen in love with the day I learned he was on the way, and I was the same mother he

29

loved and trusted. Autism couldn't dent that. I would never allow his autism to be an excuse for, or to take credit for, the facets of his being that made him whole and unique. I had a child with autism, not an autistic child. I would never put the adjective before the child.

No fan am I of gratuitous political correctness. That is not how I see "child with autism" versus "autistic." I see it as an honest confrontation of how words can be accurate and yet set up expectations or preconceived notions that seriously impede progress toward attainable long-range goals.

Parents and professionals within the autism community understand that when we use the word autistic, we mean "of or relating to autism or a person with autism." But those of us who live with and love a child with autism also live with the vexing lack of knowledge and unfair stereotypes assigned by the larger world. Whether we like it or not, "autistic" does not yet inspire favorable general reactions, does not yet stir the bystander to look beyond the label to see a whole person, splendidly full of both gifts and gaffes. The broader reaction, "Uh-oh. Silent, withdrawn hand-flapper," is too common; the first assumption is one of limitations. Or maybe we get the opposite but equally suffocating notion: "Uh-oh. Awkward, antisocial computer/math/music prodigy."

We change perceptions one person at a time. And we begin by asking ourselves: what expectations do words set up?

In the early days of my search for information that would give me some grasp of autism, I came across a ridiculous online dictionary that paired the word autistic with the synonym "unfit," and continued with a jaw-dropping list of 155 "related terms," including anesthetized, catatonic, emotionally dead, greedy, heartless, narcissistic, self-besot, soulless, and untouchable. Not one of these words described my child—nor yours, I'll bet.

In the long run—and it is a long run—what you choose to believe about a child's autism may be the single biggest factor affecting his ultimate outcome. Consciously or otherwise, you make decisions based on your perspective hundreds of times a day. Losing sight of your whole child behind a label makes your life and his more trying. All children spiral through equilibrium and disequilibrium as they cruise the developmental timeline. Most children will test limits, potty-talk in public, elevate stubbornness to Olympic proportions, flush Batman down the toilet, neglect hygiene, and cry when they don't get their way. Attributing it all to autism is not only inaccurate and unfair, it robs you of experiencing the aspects of your child's development that are typical. He has hopes, preferences, likes, dislikes, fears, and dreams like any other child. In time and with teaching, he will be able to tell you about them, albeit maybe not with words.

Every child deserves to start his or her life and education with a slate clean of preconceived notions. Even when not malicious, labels are seldom harmless. Consider the varied ways in which putting the adjective before the child colors our expectations and our children's potential.

Too low

"Bryce is getting As in my classes," a teacher told me at our first middle school parent conference. "He does everything asked of him, his homework is never late, he participates enthusiastically in class, and he is never off-task."

He continued: "Bryce has exceeded everything I thought I knew about how much autistic kids can accomplish. I've had autistic kids in my classes. His creativity and organization are far and above the others . . ."

His voice tapered off in mid-sentence. "I think I get it," he said. "That word, 'autistic,' sets up an expectation that is probably lower than what the child is capable of. Am I getting it?"

Yes, he got it, and an already-good teacher got better for every child with autism who came after Bryce. The teacher realized that when he qualified "kid" with "autistic," he set a bar in his mind for what the child couldn't do. Each person who interacts with the child sets the bar at a different place. Whether too low ("You don't think I can do it. Why try?") or too high ("I'm never good enough. Why try?"), should we force the child to travel the extra distance to meet what might be our own ill-conceived expectations? The road is long enough as it is.

Too high

"Autistic today, genius tomorrow."

When this bumper sticker loomed up in front of me on the rump of an SUV, it reminded me that messages perpetuating stereotypes, even when well-intended, are dangerous. In reinforcing a lofty clichéd characterization that most individuals with autism will never achieve, "autistic today, genius tomorrow" sets up for failure the very people it seeks to support. A middle school administrator once told me how much he enjoyed getting to know Bryce, a child with autism who was neither a genius nor a behavior problem. The fact that a seasoned educator found him remarkable is sad, isn't it? Placing the bar too high, setting up a personal or a societal expectation that any day now our child with autism will wake up as a brainiac, more likely creates a parent who motors along without a realistic grasp of the strengths and weaknesses of his/her own child, and a child who will go through life with feelings of chronic inadequacy. Imagine it—the eyes of impatient society following you, collective fingers drumming, waiting for "genius" to show itself. Whether the child is struggling or is happily adjusted to who he is, the expectation of breakthrough greatness is bound to be a(nother) heavy burden. The mother of a six-year-old told me that of all the questions she fields about her son's autism, the one that rankles most is, "What's his gift?" Some children with autism will someday manifest genius. Most will not. Some people without autism emerge as geniuses. Most do not. We owe our children faith, conviction, and support, whether or not they will display "genius tomorrow." Genius doesn't guarantee independence, productivity, or satisfaction in life. We know a young man with autism who has indeed grown up to be a math genius. His mother worries because they are a family of math geniuses—chronically unemployed math geniuses. She's seen how genius doesn't translate into ability to interact effectively with coworkers and clients, to accept direction, set goals, meet deadlines. She'd be happier if her son had a little less genius, a lot more social savvy and some marketable job skills.

Too broad

Here's a peek into my professional life, as it pertains to this discussion. Editors and instructors constantly pummel writers to avoid adjectives, instead to use stronger, more active, more descriptive nouns, verbs and phrases. Such words don't always flow from us writers; it often takes effort to pull up those more specific, more emotive terms. But it always makes for more compelling story-telling. Whether or not you're a writer, you become a story-teller on the day your child is born. How you tell your child's story at each step of his development will determine the type of people drawn to him or her. It will influence who commits to playing a role in it for a page, a chapter or longer, and who tunes out.

Looking back at dozens of IEP meetings and teacher conferences over a span of more than twenty years, I can recall very few times when I, or the seventy-five or so teachers Bryce had, discussed his autism by name. Vivid in my memory are the hundreds of hours and pages of in-depth discussion and strategizing about numerous social, academic, language and sensory issues. One by one, year by year, we defined, framed, addressed and vanquished each one in terms of measurable success, largely sans labels. In time and with teaching, Bryce learned to ask for what he needed, based on an understanding of his own learning and processing style. The label applied to that learning and processing style wasn't of primary relevance.

Autism offers few short cuts, few pat answers or glib descriptions for how we represent our child to the world he must inhabit. Through many years of day camps, swim lessons, new teachers, coaches, neighbors, or friends, I never referred to my son as autistic, but rather offered a short list of communication tactics and accommodations that would give him the best shot at success in each environment. I asked people to speak to him directly, at close range, and without slang or idioms. To show more than tell. To direct his attention to appropriate peer models. These instructions were simple but not simplistic. Those concrete directives gave other people in my son's life tools that made his concrete successes possible.

More recently, a news item caught my eye that illustrated the vastness of the spectrum of abilities within autism. A mom seeking services for her adult son said: "He is almost a savant when it comes to learning facts, but he can't use them." In high school, the young man scored ninety-two percent in pure math, but daily problem-solving gives him difficulty. This mother said it took four years to teach her son to ride the bus alone. In my house, on the other side of the spectrum, Bryce often struggles with retrieving facts, and standardized tests will always be his nemesis. But it took me one hour to teach him, at fifteen, to ride the bus alone. Ditto for many other daily life skills he wanted to learn.

In general terms, both of these young men could be called autistic. In its least damaging context, the word does little to meaningfully describe the unique challenges and needs each faces. In a more alarming context, the homogenous thinking it engenders can prevent kids from getting the individualized services they need.

Too pervasive

The increase in autism diagnoses and the rigorous efforts of parents, educators, medical professionals and advocacy organizations have succeeded in raising autism awareness in the general population to unprecedented levels. Now, the widespread use of the term "autistic" as a blanket adjective has opened the door to its abuse. In 2011, multiple instances surfaced in the Korean media of journalists applying "autistic" as a pejorative term describing uncooperative or belligerent behavior of adults, particularly politicians. A reader of mine in Europe confirmed that similar usage occurs in her country. "Autistic has become a slang word here and it shows up in a lot of media articles," she said. "The headline 'Intellectual Autism' was used to criticize a prominent professor's take on economics. Or 'autistic sexuality' to signify sex without emotional connection." In the United States, I've heard teenagers sneer, "Are you autistic?" in the context of upbraiding a peer for being momentarily tongue-tied, or for refusing to respond to jibes or provocative statements.

I resist at every turn the usage of any language that robs our children of their right to be viewed, treated, and educated as individuals with specific needs and strengths. Cultural co-option of autism stereotypes as convenient slurs adds yet another barrier to society's acceptance of our children as whole persons, and another reason to steer our language toward more specific, more edifying representations of our child.

Many children with autism will grow into adults who choose to identify themselves as autistic. Many will not ascribe to that label, or any other. In all cases, the choice should be theirs alone. Ideally, they will make it based on a childhood that began, as all childhoods should, with a blank slate of possibility. They arrive at adulthood after a moving staircase of years in which adults nurtured their skills and assets, provided education and guidance both cognitive and social-emotional, taught them informed self-advocacy and that their autism might be a reason behind some of their challenges, but never an excuse or free pass.

So run the word "autistic" through your reality-checker and ask yourself if it in any way limits your view of what the future holds for your child or student with autism and the value he brings to your world. If it does, remember that nothing, *nothing*, is predetermined and that your time together brims with open-ended opportunity.

Chapter Two

My senses are out of sync.

Sensory integration may be the most difficult aspect of autism to understand, but it's arguably the most critical. Cognitive and social learning cannot break through to a child whose world is intrusively loud, blindingly bright, unbearably malodorous and physically complicated to navigate. His brain cannot filter multiple sensory inputs and he frequently feels overloaded, disoriented, and unsettled in his own skin.

And into this shrieking, blinding hurricane of sensory acid rain we insert the expectation that this child "pay attention," "behave," learn, adhere to social rules that mystify her, and communicate with us. Neglect a child's sensory challenges and you will never get close to discovering her capability. Sensory issues are that crucial to her overall ability to function.

Picture yourself on the world's hippest roller coaster. (If you dislike roller coasters, this makes the example even better.) Coney Island and Six Flags are fun vacation venues, but how long could you do your day job while ensconced on the Cyclone, the Xcelerator or the Kingda Ka? Could you conduct that meeting, teach that class, be charming dinner company, write the report and clean the house while enduring the vertigo, the screams of fellow riders, the g-force of the rushing air, the unexpected drops and abrupt changes of direction, the sensation of hair in your mouth and bugs in your teeth? It might be fun as an occasional thrill, but admit it—you want to get off after the three-minute ride. For many children with autism, it's a ride with no exit gate, a 24/7 affair and the very antithesis of thrilling.

It's natural that we shy away from concepts and conditions that demand arduous effort to comprehend, that we seek easier solutions. For the nonprofessional, gaining a working understanding of how sensory integration issues affect a particular child can be downright intimidating. An area of immense complexity, it pervades everything we do or try to do. That's why it's the first outpost of autism we should address. It sends me off the deep end when I hear sensory therapy described as an add-on, or something to try after everything else has failed. Or that our children's sensory issues aren't real, or are "all in their heads."

It's all in their heads, all right. Science has long recognized that sensory integration takes place in the brainstem, and that sensory integrative dysfunction causes what amounts to a traffic pile-up in the brain. You may already be looking right at the manifestation of sensory overload and not recognize it. Hands over the ears is an obvious indication. Less obvious but no less compelling are the behaviors referred to as stims, self-stimulating conduct such as rocking, chewing, flapping, rubbing, wandering, and other repetitive mannerisms. Seemingly inexplicable behavior such as aggression, excessive silliness, clumsiness, and over- or underreaction to injury can have an underlying sensory cause. In the case of more extreme behavior such as meltdowns, the trigger may not be obvious; nevertheless, sensory overload should be the first suspect brought in for questioning. That questioning can be tricky, intricate, and protracted. But one of the few universal truths about autism is this: no matter how unprovoked, how random it may appear, behavior never, ever comes out of nowhere. There is always a detonator (and we will discuss this at length in Chapter Nine). Find it you must, and keep in mind that if your child is nonverbal or has limited verbal skills, she will not be able to tell you what is causing such discomfort. Even your chatterbox child with Asperger's, who seems so verbally competent, may not have the vocabulary or awareness sophisticated enough to describe what is happening within her complicated neurology.

Developing a practical understanding of sensory integration can be challenging. As many as twenty-one sensory systems are at work in our bodies. You're familiar with the predominant five: visual (sight), auditory (sound), tactile (touch), olfactory (smell), and gustatory (taste). Five other senses are commonly attributed to humans: equilibrioception (sense of balance or vestibular sense), proprioception and kinesthesia (sensing the orientation and motion of one's limbs and body in space), nociciption (pain), temporal sense (sense of time), and thermoception (temperature differences). When any of these senses fall out of calibration, they can wreak havoc in your child's life.

Comprehensive discussion of the sensory systems is beyond the scope of this chapter. What follows here is a short description of each sense and what its dysfunction can mean for the child with autism. Hyperacute sensory systems call for calming overloaded senses. But senses can also be hypoacute, or underresponsive. The need in those cases is to alert, not calm, the underresponding sense. An occupational therapist, an indispensable member of any child's autism team, can elaborate upon and address your child or student's individual issues. Bear in mind, too, that acuity may not be the same across all the child's senses. Some may be hyper, some may be hypo, and some can vary from day to day, even hour to hour.

The visual sense

For many children with autism, the visual sense is their strongest. The good news/bad news is that while they rely more heavily upon visual input to learn and to navigate their world, it can be the first sense to become overstimulated. Bright lights or objects, reflective surfaces, too many objects in the field of vision or objects moving at fast or irregular speeds can cause distortion and sensory chaos. So pervasive is this sense for many children with autism that it warrants its own discussion later in the book.

We'll note here though that while the visual sense may be the most robust in many children with autism, there will be some for whom the visual sense is underactive or disorganized. This may manifest itself in a child who sways or rocks (attempting to change angle of visual perspective), is leery of changes in elevation (ladders, stairs), or becomes fascinated with moving objects (model trains, water wheels). Physical limitations may also be in play. Some children may lack depth perception, have limited fields of vision (think of looking through a paper towel tube and missing everything else around you), or the visual picture of their world may look distorted and fragmented, like a Picasso painting.

The auditory sense

Our auditory sense provides us with a tremendous amount of information. We take in and instantly interpret the component qualities of sound—volume, pitch, frequency, vibration—and the directionality of it. We turn our head to seek out voices, footsteps, and traffic. When hearing is typically calibrated, we perk up and attend to whispers to glean what's being said, and only the loudest sounds will cause us to recoil, cover our ears, or otherwise protect ourselves.

For many individuals with autism, the auditory sense is the most commonly impaired. Hyperacute hearing can cause agonizing pain. The sounds of an average day are too loud, too high-pitched, too sudden, too sharp, too intrusive. The child with autism may hear things undetectable to your ear, escalating an already overwhelming world into deafening dissonance. She likely lacks the ability to suppress and/or filter sound, to distinguish your voice over the sound of the dryer or the television, or the teacher's voice over the murmurs and movements of others in the classroom. Environments that appear orderly to the casual observer may be a confusing minefield of clatter for the child with auditory hypersensitivity.

Obvious too-loud flags like blaring music, gymnasium basketball, cafeteria and playground cacophony, and emergency vehicle sirens are examples of everyday commotion that can induce physical pain. Sudden loud sounds such as fire drills or cars backfiring can trigger a level of panic from which your child may take hours to recover. In extreme examples, the child has been able to hear the heartbeats of others in the room. As for enjoying the pounding surf at the beach, forget surf. Think pounding, as in headache.

Less apparent but as invasive or intolerable are ordinary, seemingly non-threatening noises. He's not hiding in his room because he doesn't like his family; he's fleeing the dissonance of the dishwasher, coffeemaker, washer, dryer, leaf blower, television, and teen-on-the-cellphone all having their say at once. He might as well be right inside that spin cycle himself. Over at school, his peers in the classroom listen as the teacher speaks. But the child with autism cannot identify the voice of the teacher as the primary sound to which he should be attuned. To him it's indistinguishable from the grinding of the pencil sharpener, the fly buzzing on the windowsill, the lawn mower chugging outside, the child with the constant cough behind him, and the class next door tromping down the hall to the library.

Well-known author Temple Grandin, who writes and speaks extensively about her own experiences as a person with autism, puts this succinct grace note on it: "Wal-Mart is like being inside the speaker at a rock concert."

Hypoacute hearing brings its own brand of trouble. It impacts language development and use, social learning, and academics. Children may miss pieces of what's being said, be unable to process certain types of sounds, or may perceive what they hear as long strings of sounds rather than individual words and phrases. What looks like laziness or noncompliance may be a sensory impairment that prevents them from filtering and/or processing the ordinary sounds of daily life.

The child with an understimulated auditory sense also struggles to process information coming from sound. He may speak too softly or too loudly, seek out noisy appliances (lawn mowers, hair dryers, blenders), or environments for additional sensory input, handle toys and other objects roughly to create crashing noises, exhibit fascination with rushing water (waterfalls, running bathwater, flushing toilets), or like vibrating/buzzing toys.

Whether over- or understimulated, suspect auditory processing difficulties if your child or student can follow written or visual directives well, but struggles with or is unable to comprehend oral instruction.

The tactile sense

Our skin registers an astonishing amount of information: light touches as well as deeper pressure, a wide range of temperatures, different types of pain or irritation, vibration and other movement, and textures ranging from slimy to rough.

Hypersensitivity to touch is called tactile defensiveness. The child with autism, trapped in her own skin, is unable to regulate distressing sensations that rain upon her in the form of uncomfortable clothes, unwelcome touches from other people (hugs that might seem warm and friendly to you might be torture to her) and unpleasant textures of things she is confronted with touching or eating.

For the tactile-defensive child, clothing tags, buttons, zippers, elastic around wrists or necks, and similar clothing embellishments cause constant distraction. Whether indoors or out, going barefoot is not an option (do you have a tip-toe walker in your house?). The child may evade your embrace, and fight like a badger against haircuts, shampooing, teeth brushing, and nail clipping. Hands-on tasks like finger-painting and sand table activities may induce more stress than fun.

Hyposensitivity results in the child who craves tactile sensation. She is the child who runs her hand along the wall walking from class to class, must touch everyone and everything, or may not be affected by temperature shifts. She may exhibit perplexing, even disturbing behavior, sometimes bordering on danger. She may stim to the point of hurting herself (biting, pinching, applying pressure with various objects, brushing teeth too hard), unaware of the intensity of her actions and her high threshold to pain and temperature. She may prefer tight, heavy, or textured clothing, or engage in odd activities such as taking a bath fully clothed. She may purposely touch or bump into objects and other people to enliven her senses, then eventually shy away from trying new motor activities because she may be perceived by others as clumsy. Because children with hypotactile processing seek constant contact, parents may characterize them as clingy and others may find their touches invasive and inappropriate.

Most occupational therapists will tell you how successful they can be at desensitizing a hyperacute tactile sense or awakening a hypoacute sense. Take it from a mom whose child spent the early years of his life sporting only his birthday suit whenever he could get away with it and doling out backwards hugs (facing away) to a precious few. By third grade he chose jeans and flannel shirts. By fifth grade he had hiked, biked, backpacked, and white-watered the Great Outdoors with all kinds of slimy-crawly critters and substances without batting an eye. That's what's possible with appropriate and regular intervention.

The olfactory sense

"Ewwwww, what stinks?" is a common refrain in our household, often when my nose detects nothing. Paraeducators have told me that their students with autism greet them with "You smell funny!" though they are fresh from the shower. Olfactory defensiveness (hyperacute sense of smell) is common among children with autism. Aromas, scents, and fragrances regarded by the typical population as pleasant or undetectable have the power to make the child with autism miserable, even ill. If a certain paint, glue, perfume, or floor cleaner has ever given you an instant headache, if the smell of fish, broccoli, garlic, cat food, or limburger cheese has ever turned your stomach or brought tears to your eyes, multiply that sensation many times over and you'll get an inkling of what your child may be experiencing. Don't ask your child to change the kitty litter box. That "odor free"/natural citrus/recycled pine concoction, combined with the you-know-what that lurks within, will knock the poor kid back into yesterday.

Years ago, Bryce's olfactory issues nearly derailed a long-anticipated trip to Disneyland when it had barely begun. In an effort to keep everything as familiar as possible, we had booked a rental car of the same make and model as our car at home. I told Bryce that a car like ours would be waiting at the end of our plane trip to take us to the hotel. Having (still!) underestimated his literal thinking, I realized too late that he pictured our own car coming out of the cargo hold along with our luggage. The rental car, though indeed the same make and model as our car, came with a horrible twist—it was new. Now, for many people, that new car smell ranks right up there with cinnamon buns and baby powder as a favorite. For Bryce, it was a show-stopper. "This is a SMELLY car!" he decreed. "A SMELLY, SMELLY CAR!" It took an eternity to get him into the car, and another eternity of listening to the SMELLY CAR! mantra all the way into town. Do I need to tell you we took the hotel shuttle to the park the next day?

Here are a Dirty Dozen of potential olfactory offenders in the home:

scented laundry products (if it's on his clothes, he can't get away from it), scented soaps and shampoos (includes kid scents, such as bubble gum), bathroom air fresheners (they only add another layer of odor), hand lotions, deodorants, aftershaves, body gels, hair products, house-cleaning products such as ammonia, bleach, other fragranced cleaners, cooking odors, and yard-and-garden chemicals.

In the school setting, we have the paint area, odiferous science projects, the classmate wearing cologne, the old oil-burning furnace or the window that opens onto the newly-mowed, composting lawn, the hamster cage and the days-old forgotten lunch in the closet. More than one student with autism has been known to experience the uncontrollable gag reflex in the cafeteria. (Offer an alternative place to eat lunch if lunchtime smells disturb your student.)

An understimulated olfactory sense shows itself in a child who may seem overinterested in sniffing his own body and others. She may put unusual nonfood items in her mouth such as dirt, paste, coins, or soap, or she may exhibit lack of sensitivity to odors others consider offensive, such as urine (bedwetting) and feces (smearing). Both of the foregoing can also be signs of an understimulated tactile sense.

The gustatory sense

Our sense of taste ties closely to the olfactory sense. The olfactory sense acts as a kind of sentry: if a potential food item smells dangerous—moldy, burnt, rancid, or otherwise "off" we don't put it in our mouths. It's nature's way of protecting us from ingesting poisons and toxins. A person's olfactory sensations can alter the flavor of a substance. "The components that comprise the sensation of flavor include the food's smell, taste, texture, and temperature," writes otolaryngologist Donald Leopold on http://emedicine.medscape.com. "Each of these sensory modalities is stimulated independently to produce a distinct flavor when food enters the mouth."

A hyperacute gustatory system reacts with increased sensitivity to pungent tastes like bitterness (such as the phytochemicals found in many vegetables) and heat (spicy foods containing capsaicin, such as chili). It may also reject foods based on temperature or texture; the child may shun cold foods (ice cream or refrigerated juice), oozy/slippery foods (puddings, canned peaches, condiments),or mixed-consistency foods, such as casseroles, sandwiches, or soups. The grainy texture of meat frequently offends, as may carbonated drinks (this is a plus, isn't it?). The result is that many children with autism or Asperger's are selective eaters to a breathtaking degree, sometimes limiting themselves to only a few foods.

On the other end of the sensitivity scale is the hypotaster. This child may have a reduced perception of taste, and may 1) eat everything in sight because it all tastes good, 2) eat little because food as a pleasant sensory experience has no meaning or interest, 3) eat unusual taste combinations of food (e.g. pickles and ice cream, French fries dipped in peach yogurt, peanut butter on a hot dog), or 4) eat a horrifying array of nonfood items, like dirt, clay, glue, coffee grounds, dust bunnies, and paper.

Underlying physiological problems, such as mineral deficiencies, can also alter a child's sense of taste, as can poor oral hygiene, which also can lead to viral or bacterial infections.

The health implications for both supertasters and hypotasters are troubling. The hypertasters reject many of the foods providing the highest health benefits, like vegetables. The hypotasters are susceptible to just the opposite, the excesses of oral gratification and illnesses associated with overeating and, later in their adult life, alcohol and smoking.

Addressing gustatory sensitivities requires time and patience. For the sake of your own sanity, "don't try this at home" without the advice of an occupational therapist.

The vestibular and proprioceptive senses

Like a well-run corporate accounting office, these two critical but little understood senses get no attention when everything is running smoothly. Only when things go awry do we become aware of the mayhem created when an essential piece of infrastructure malfunctions.

The vestibular system regulates the sense of equilibrium (balance, stability) by responding to changes in the position of the eyes and head. Its command center is located in the inner ear. The proprioceptive sense uses feedback from joints and muscles to tell us where our body is in space and what forces and pressures are acting upon it. Because vestibular and proprioceptive problems are not easily recognized by the untrained eye, the danger is that they go unidentified and untreated, leaving the child with autism to cope unaided within a very hostile environment.

Impairments to the vestibular and proprioceptive senses can hamper or halt everyday motor functions. The child may trip over her own feet, bounce off walls, and fall out of chairs. She may experience gravitational insecurity, becoming anxious in settings that take her feet off solid ground, such as climbing the steps to the slide, using a public toilet, riding a bike and sitting on a too-tall chair or stool without a footrest. Anxieties about managing fundamental movements can be magnified by the additional expectation that she learn new skills, whether cognitive/academic, social or gross motor. In this regard, it's easy to understand why many children with autism or Asperger's shy away from sports, with its overwhelming multiple expectations: assume certain positions, have the gross motor skills and motor planning ability to execute sequential moves such as diving for the ball, catching it, jumping up and throwing it, or to dribble, aim, and shoot a basketball. Then add in the social cognitive elements: remember the rules, apply the rules, and communicate with teammates (get bawled out by teammates and adults when you blow a play).

Vestibular disorder can affect nearly every function of the body, causing a dizzying (no pun intended) range of symptoms including, but not limited to, loss of balance, chronic nausea, distorted hearing (ears may feel stuffed, or sound may come across as full of static, like bad radio reception), and visual disturbances (objects or printed material appears to be blurry or in motion). Distance focus may be difficult, glare from lights may seem exaggerated, and the child may suffer difficulty with memory and/or focus, chronic fatigue, acute anxiety. and depression.

Children with proprioceptive dysfunction may walk with an odd, heavy gait, have trouble with tableware, pencils, and other fine motor implements, lose their balance when their eyes are closed, or be "crashers," forever running into or jumping off things as they seek deep pressure sensory input.

In addition to that indispensable occupational therapist, an adapted physical education (APE) specialist can help with large motor issues, modifying curriculum and equipment so your child can participate with his peers in PE and playground activities. Ask if your school district has a special education motor team or APE consultant.

Concerted effort

Most children on the autism spectrum struggle with more than one sensory challenge. The type and extent of the impairment (hyper in one, hypo in another, or any combination) can shift and change, day to day, over time, and with treatment. "Concerted" has two meanings—strenuous, and collaborative. To alleviate the very authentic sensory challenges our children face, they need from us concerted effort in both its definitions. Team tactics, with parents, school, and therapist all working together, will produce the greatest results.

One of the occupational therapist's most effective tools is a child-specific plan of action called the sensory diet, sometimes called a sensory map. A sensory diet or map identifies a child's particular sensory needs and prescribes regularly scheduled activities that help him organize sensory input in a manner that makes it easier to engage, attend, and self-regulate. Through formal and informal observation and evaluation, your OT will determine three components:

- The child's level of sensory arousal as it fluctuates throughout the day. Low arousal/hyposensitivity requires alerting inputs. Overarousal/hypersensitivity requires calming inputs.
- Current state of the child's sensory systems (which senses are strong and which are challenged).
- Documentation to determine the source of the sensory

challenge, of specific incidents that set off emotional or behavioral responses (transitions, certain activities, locations or people, having to deal with certain substances).

The primary goals of sensory therapy are to teach the child the self-awareness to recognize sensory issues as they arise, then to learn and employ self-regulation strategies or request help when self-regulation isn't possible. These might include regularly scheduled movement breaks, providing fidget or chew toys, and providing a study carrel or quiet corner.

A primary goal of sensory therapy is to help the child learn to self-recognize sensory issues as they arise and then use sensory smart strategies (taught beforehand) to self-regulate or request help when that isn't possible. Embedding into his day activities that both address his needs and play to his strengths will give him a sense of control and can-do that heightens his ability to engage both cognitively and socially.

Sensory processing dysfunction isn't exclusive to autism, and it may help you understand your child's needs if you reflect upon your own and those of the people around you. In Carol Kranowitz's lighthearted but revealing children's book *The Goodenoughs Get in Sync,* every family member right down to the dog works to cope with a different set of sensory processing difficulties. Dad can't tell the difference between grape and strawberry jellies, nor can he judge which of two shovels is heavier. Mom must always be "touching things, moving around, stretching, humming, chewing, fiddling with pencil, chalk or rubber band." The children describe their struggles with fight-flight-freeze response, their difficulty articulating, their gravitational insecurity, visual defensiveness, audio discrimination, dyspraxia, and other motor-based difficulties. When the family members ignore their sensory needs, the household descends into chaos. But when they resume their sensory-diet activities, equilibrium returns. Each tells his or her own story and as you might guess, the children's voices are riveting.

Forget the Pyramid of Giza and the Hanging Gardens of Babylon, the real Wonders of the World are the neurological senses whose function or dysfunction hold such profound power over us. Seven years of devoted sensory training helped my wordless, aggressive toddler grow into a confident and kind-hearted scholar, artist, athlete, and fun tween. Now that's a monument.

Chapter Three

Distinguish between won't (I choose not to) and can't (I am not able to).

Is a zebra white with black stripes or black with white stripes? Ask ten people or pull up ten websites and you'll get twelve opinions. Zebras give the impression of being white with black stripes because the stripes end without joining under the belly and around the legs. But the hide of the zebra is actually black. It's a lesson from Mother Nature that things are not always as they appear on the surface.

And so it is with many of the complexities of autism. How do we distinguish between what our child won't do (chooses not to) and what he can't do (is not able to)? Many "won't" allegations about our kids are behavior complaints. He won't comply; she won't listen to instructions;

he won't stop rapping his knuckles, walking away in mid-sentence or other odd, inexplicable or narrowly focused actions. We adults assume comprehension (functional and social), assume that because he did something once, he can repeat the behavior without further prompting, practice, or reinforcement, under all circumstances. As adults do with so many challenges our children face, we make all sorts of assumptions about knowledge and ability without stopping to consider that our assumptions may be the root of the problem at hand.

"Won't" and "can't" are not interchangeable. "Won't," the contraction of "will not," implies premeditation, intent, and deliberate behavior. "Can't," the contraction of "can not," acknowledges that a behavior is not a matter of choice, but attributable to lack of ability, knowledge, or opportunity.

The distinction between "can't" and "won't" is clear-cut, because where behavior is concerned, there are two absolutes.

- All behavior is communication.
- All behavior happens for a reason.

Today's psychology recognizes varied motives for behavior: bids for attention, sensory seeking or avoidance, feelings of powerlessness, testing boundaries, experimentation at different stages of cognitive and social development, explorations into independence, and many others. Some may be the direct result of challenges arising from autism; others may be developmental stages that all children, autism or not, pass through. The next time you catch yourself saying, "He won't. . ." stop and evaluate your child's behavior in light of the following more common reasons. See if you start recognizing situations where "can't" is a more accurate description than "won't."

Resistant/avoidant behavior. Your child or student doesn't know how to do what you've asked or it's unpleasant to him for a reason you don't perceive.

It's natural for a child (or adult) to want to evade an unpleasant task. Pinpointing the source of the resistance is necessary to resolving it. Your essential role is now behavior detective. You may be surprised at how often lack of ability, information, or opportunity plays into your child's or student's reluctance or refusal to do what you have asked; think "close to 100% of the time." Possible reasons (get coffee; we'll be here a while): he didn't hear your request or only pieces filtered through to his brain, he doesn't comprehend the instructions/the request, doesn't know or understand the rules/process/routine, doesn't have the fine or gross motor skills to accomplish the task, the behavioral or academic expectation is too high, the activity is sensory-overwhelming, the task causes physical discomfort or the request comes at a time when he is hungry or too tired to comply. In other words, he can't.

On top of that, he dreads failure and criticism. In his concrete, black-and-white, all-or-nothing perspective, errors and successes come in two sizes: huge or nonexistent. This breeds pervasive stress and anxiety in him. Further, have you offered choice or flexibility in how and when he must accomplish the task? Has he had any say in how he could best tackle it?

Avoidance behaviors frequently stem from lack of comprehension and fear of failure. Constructing opportunities within which children experience success motivates them to try, to work, to strive.

Attention-seeking behavior. Your child wants adult or peer attention.

The good news is, he wants to interact. The bad news is that inappropriate attention-seeking behavior frequently disrupts classrooms and family routine. If you're exasperated because he "won't" stop, get out the deerstalker again and consider: does he know how to ask for attention or help in an appropriate manner? It's one of autism's nasty Catch 22s that the child must be carefully taught about social interaction, but at the same time lacks the understanding of when and how to ask for what he needs. He needs specific instruction and examples to make requests such as "I need help" or "I don't understand this," and he needs emotional bolstering while he learns to summon not just the words or actions, but the courage to ask. While teaching him to ask for attention appropriately, also consider whether he may not get sufficient adult attention to achieve what's expected of him. Similarly, does he receive adequate and appropriate attention from peers to validate his self-worth? Does he draw more attention from you for his undesirable deeds than he does for the more suitable behaviors? Is the amount of praise he hears from you greater than the amount of complaining? (A 4:1 praise-criticism ratio is widely advocated by educators and psychologists.) Do you unknowingly reinforce the behaviors you want to quell? If you ignore her when she's not being disruptive but take immediate notice when the spitballs sail or she uses the sofa as a trampoline, she's gotten the attention she wanted, and you've succeeded in reinforcing her inappropriate behaviors. Remember our maxim: all behavior is communication. It applies to you, too.

Self-regulation. As we discussed in Chapter Two, your child unconsciously attempts to calm or alert over- or understimulated senses to reduce anxiety or discomfort. This may be the underlying organic cause of a behavior, and until we help the child through sensory intervention and teach him sensory strategies to use, such behavior falls into the "I can't" category.

Entertainment/fun. Your child finds a particular behavior amusing to himself or others.

While children with autism or Asperger's often have a more rigid or reduced sense of play than typical kids, they can also be resourceful at entertaining themselves. It's a grand skill, as any mother of an "I'm bored. There's nothing to do" kid will tell you. If your child repeats the diverting behaviors when others are not present, it may be his way of telling you he wants to play but has neither adequate skill nor the opportunity to interact with other children. The door is open, Coach. Set up a game plan.

Control. Your child is attempting to order or reorder his environment.

When so little is within their control, many children on the autism spectrum experience life as a continuous battle to hold onto whatever power they do have to direct their lives. Their attempts to control may be overt (confrontational, aggressive behavior that looks like defiance), or they may be passive-aggressive (they silently or covertly continue to do what they wish regardless of attempts at redirecting behavior).

Your daily life as a typical adult flows in a perpetual, minute-by-minute stream of choices. You take for granted both the array of choices you have and your ability to act upon them. Such reasoning and decision-making skills are much more limited in your child with autism. What appears to be controlling behavior on your child's part can also be seen as evidence of her ability to think independently and affirm her own wants and needs. Channel these qualities as you work with her to instill decision-making skills and increase the number of choices and opportunities for success in her world.

It's too easy to get into a power struggle with a child who seems hell-bent on having things his way, but always remind yourself of your goals for this child before you respond. Is your goal to bend the child to your will, make him respect your authority, and force his compliance at all costs? (Ask yourself if that really is a win.) Or is the goal to acclimate him to socially acceptable behavior in a manner that enables him to grow as a person and take his place as a citizen of the world? As a young child, Bryce had a passive-aggressive manner of letting us know when he had had enough of a social situation: he would tell us—once. If we did not end the outing within a timeframe reasonable to him (less than five minutes), he would simply turn and go. Depending upon where we were, you can imagine how dangerous this could be. I still break out in hives remembering those times, his little back disappearing down the street or into the crowd. We quickly learned that when Bryce said, "I'm ready to go," that meant nonnegotiable, *arrivederci* time. Was he pulling our strings? Were we letting him run the show? Not by a long shot. He was telling us that he was approaching his meltdown point. We respected that, ungrudgingly, and adapted our plans accordingly. Our goal was that Bryce be able to handle social settings in a manner that would allow us to do things as an entire family. To accomplish that goal, we had to learn to listen and heed his verbal and nonverbal warnings when he reached the limits of his current abilities. We beat numerous hasty retreats in those days, but over time Bryce gained language, confidence, sensory tolerance, and social skills. We did it his way, and by his teens, we had a go-anywhere young man who got around town on his own and, to celebrate his high school graduation, traveled across the country solo.

Retribution. Your child wants to retaliate for treatment perceived as unfair.

I include this one here because it's most likely a motivation you can rule out.

"He's doing it to get back at me." Let it go, my friend. The concept of fair/unfair requires the ability to perceive the motivations and feelings of others, something children with autism notoriously lack. What's more, planning and carrying out revenge requires advanced executive skills coupled with a level of motor planning beyond the abilities of most children on the spectrum. Keep looking. Your answer isn't here.

Once we understand how "can't" shapes our child's behavior, we must turn the word on ourselves, because "can't" is a two-faced monster. "Can't" comes in two flavors, and it sits on a very different place on the tongue when "can't" comes from you rather than your child. You, as a capable adult, do not get off the hook with "can't." As we have defined it, "can't" reflects lack of knowledge, ability, and opportunity. I am the first to acknowledge that autism demands a huge learning curve, but we're talking at a deeper level here, about playing the hand you've been dealt. It's not about backing away from difficulty and challenge in the face of your own insecurities. You didn't get a choice about the nature part of your child, but the nurture part grants you choices without number. Your child will be an expression of his environment. What vibe does he get from you? Are you a can-do adult?

One of the greatest shifts I've seen since entering the autism community is in the proactive attitudes and participation of dads and stepdads, grandfathers and uncles, the men in a child's life. When I first ventured out to speak to groups, there were virtually no dads in the audience, and I rarely received an email from a dad. With the virulent increase in autism diagnosis and awareness has come the willingness of many male family members to step out of the grief, denial, and fear that often haunts them following a child's diagnosis. They now head support groups, chair fund raisers, write books, produce videos, software and applications, form non-profit groups, and coach teams so their kids can participate. They come to my talks and they ask piercing questions. Autism—it's not just for moms anymore! Surprisingly, it's been dads who've had the courage to vocalize one of the core insecurities some of us silently confess to ourselves, often with a heavy sidecar of guilt:

"I can't handle the day-to-dayness of it."

Two stories illuminate the can't-versus-won't attitudes many adults hold about dealing with a child's autism. The characters may be fathers, but the feelings cross all age, gender, and cultural boundaries.

I met a dad at the first autism support group meeting I ever attended. He described the meltdowns, the nonresponsiveness, the stims, and the food peculiarities. "My wife is much better at handling those things than I am. I'm focusing on providing financially for the family and realizing that I must do so for my child, lifelong. I'm working on setting that up." My immediate reaction was that his wife was going to be mighty tired.

Later I understood and gave him credit for owning up to his limitations, and trying to build constructive compensation. He accepted that his plans and goals as a parent would be different than he originally envisioned them. Not bad, just different. He wasn't in denial of his child's autism, but in the midst of his own grieving process and working through it. Because of that, this dad's can't-handle-it attitude could, in time, evolve into can-and-will, allowing him to achieve that deeper connection which could make a critical difference in his son's life.

Contrast him with another dad I met through a friend, a dad stuck like a broken record on an anti-government rant about how, by mandating vaccines for school attendance, he had been robbed of his son. "I simply can't relate to him," he sighed. "How do you think it feels to know that he'll probably end up in jail?" It's a scary, helpless feeling to be weighed down by regrets and broken dreams. But he had crossed the line from can't (am not able to) into won't (I choose not to) with the decision to look only backward into what-might-have-been, rather than forward into possibilities yet unexplored. Regardless of whether a vaccination is liable for his son's condition—and I won't (choose not to) debate that subject in this book or anywhere else—it's an after-the-fact discussion. The child can't (proper use of the word here) be un-vaccinated. By adopting a defeatist attitude rather than the more work-intensive proactive approach to help his child achieve his full potential, this dad also chose paralysis, fear, exasperation and self-fulfilling prophecy. His son was eight years old, a bright, articulate, clever, and resourceful child. He was also aggressive, angry, and frustrated—like Dad. A lifetime of "can't" messages can plant the germ of despair in a child. Or worse.

I suggested to this father that he try to reframe "can't." Your son can't change that he has autism. He can't find his way to something better unless the adults around him step up to help.

I told this father that I knew him to be more capable and caring than that. And I asked him, as my pediatrician used to ask me, who is the adult here? Who has the power to change things? Can you? With help and education you can be the teacher and guide in your child's life. Will you? He had yet to answer that question for himself.

The irony and the poignancy of can't vs. won't is that we adults often kill the very thing we want most dearly to achieve. If you yearn for a confident, optimistic, curious and engaged child, you must model those qualities and you must find and reinforce them in your child, however tiny the increment of gain. Think carefully about the role of reinforcement in your relationship with your child or student. The nuances may be subtle, but the manner in which you respond to your child's actions, words, or attitude amounts to either endorsement or denunciation. Watch what you reinforce; be sure it's something you want him or her to repeat. When you take on a can-do attitude, he can-do, too.

If you find yourself governed by thoughts such as, I can't give this child special treatment, I can't put extra time into modifying assignments or environments, and I can't do anything about the way this kid is, then you can't expect to see positive changes. Thoughtfully constructing the child's world in a manner that ensures a flow of successes, however bite-sized they may be, builds a foundation that buries the won'ts beneath it. That's not special treatment. It's what we like to think of as "the right way."

Think back to those pre-Cambrian days before you had a child. You went to a bar after work and called it Happy Hour or Attitude-Adjustment Hour. This isn't much different. You choose to make a

conscious shift in your mental state. If you don't like the boozy con-
notation, think of it as energy resource management: how much time
and energy do you expend dwelling on what you don't have and can't
have because of your child's autism? That's called brooding. How much
could you accomplish if you redirected that energy into doing, trying,
and reaching forward? That's called progress.

Chapter Four

I am a concrete thinker.
I interpret language literally.

Whatever command of your native language you thought you had will be seriously tested by your literal minded child or student with autism. You will be taken at your word to a degree you've never had to confront before. British Olympic medalist Doug Larson sums up the pitfalls of colloquial communication with the woeful assertion, "If the English language made any sense, a catastrophe would be an apostrophe with fur."

To children with autism, with their concrete, visual thinking, their (sometimes brilliant) associative abilities and, for many, their limited vocabularies, the imagery generated by common idioms and other figures of speech must be very disturbing. Ants in his pants? Butterflies in her stomach? Open a can of worms? Cat got your tongue?

It's enough to make them want to drive the porcelain bus. (Like that one? It means throw up—er—vomit.)

That imagery they conjure up is at the root of some of our everyday expressions. When you tell him it's raining cats and dogs, you mean it's raining hard. One interpretation of the origin of this idiom goes back to the English floods of the seventeenth and eighteenth centuries. After torrential downpours, the bodies of drowned cats and dogs littered the streets. It appeared as if they had rained from the skies.

And I am sure this is what many young ones with autism visualize when you say it's raining cats and dogs. "I don't see them!" fretted one little boy. "It only looks like falling-down water!" Heaven help you if he hears you telling someone it's a dog-eat-dog world, that you toasted the bride and groom, or that you warned someone not to throw the baby out with the bathwater.

You wouldn't dream of issuing instructions to your child in a foreign language, but English can seem that way. A popular Internet essay notes: "There is no egg in eggplant, neither apple nor pine in pineapple. A guinea pig is neither from Guinea nor is it a pig. If the plural of tooth is teeth, why isn't the plural of booth beeth? One goose, two geese. So one moose, two meese? If teachers taught, why haven't preachers praught? We have noses that run and feet that smell. How can a slim chance and a fat chance be the same, while a wise man and a wise guy are opposites?"

The lunacy continues with homographs. The nurse wound gauze around the wound. Farms produce produce. The birds scattered, and the dove dove into the woods. When you get close to the window, close it. Lead me to the lead pipe. Go polish the Polish table. Can you wind your watch in the wind?

Communicating with a literal-thinking child requires that we pause to consider our phrasing. It may take some retraining—yours, not his. In time, with maturity and education, the concrete-thinking child can acclimate to some degree of recognizing idioms and inferential language. While he is young and his receptive language challenges many, don't add to his befuddlement. Watch for common snags like these:

Idioms and clichés

Don't say	Instead say
You are the apple of my eye.	I love you very much.
I'm at the end of my rope.	I'm getting angry.
Bite your tongue.	Don't speak to me like that.
Let's call it a day.	It's time to stop for now.
I smell a rat.	This doesn't seem right to me.

Nonspecific instructions

Say exactly what you mean and don't make your child or student figure out nonspecific instructions.

Don't say	Instead say
Hang it over there.	Hang your coat on the hook by the door.

Don't say	Instead say
Stay out of the street.	Stop your bike at the end of the driveway.
Quit kicking.	Keep your feet under your desk.
Let's get going.	We're going home now.

Inferences

Similar to the nonspecific instruction, an inference comes across to the child with autism as merely a statement of fact. Don't make him guess. Specify the action you want him to take.

Don't say	Instead say
Your room's a mess.	Hang up your clothes.
You didn't turn your homework in.	Put your book report on my desk.
It's too cold outside.	Wear long pants instead of shorts today.
I don't like that noise.	Turn down the sound on the TV.

Phrasal Verbs

Phrasal verbs combine a verb with a preposition or adverb to form common expressions that can be as confusing as idioms to the concrete thinker.

Don't say	Instead say
We look up to him.	We admire him; he sets a good example.
The car is acting up.	The car (or part of the car) is not working right.
Jamie got kicked out of class.	The teacher sent Jamie to talk with the principal.
Let's wrap this up.	It's time to stop playing trains.

By now you have an inkling of how much of our everyday conversation is imprecise and, to the child with autism, illogical. You'll learn even more quickly the first time you tell him to "wait just a minute for me" and he's not there when you come back in five.

And while we're on the subject of sloppy talk, expecting a child with autism to follow teenage conversation is ludicrous. "We was talking and stuff, and I'm, like, I am SO not going there. And he just went, okay whatever, and I'm like FINE. Like I could care less, and then he goes, like, yeah bite me." Parents and teachers! It's more than okay to require siblings and classmates to speak comprehensible English around individuals with autism. Translated, the foregoing passage would sound like this: "I didn't want to talk with Jake anymore. We were both saying unkind things." Remember the scene in that irreverent old movie *Airplane*? "Pardon me, Stewardess, I speak jive." If different dialects, accents, and cadences of your own native language can be confusing to you, think of what a Tower of Babel they are to the child with autism.

To have a child who struggled with language was the ultimate irony for me. My college diploma reads, Bachelor of Science, Speech Communication. The top shelf of our garage houses a crate of gently rusting high school debate trophies. Yes, I am a certified windbag. I come from a family of inveterate punsters and wordmeisters, forever dreaming up obscure word games. I trod a major learning curve to, first, realize my child wasn't capable of or interested in this kind of verbal jousting, and second, accept that if I wanted to communicate meaningfully with him (and oh, how I did), I would have to rework my own manner of presentation. I had to think before I spoke. I had to carefully choose my words, my tone of voice, my inflection. If I didn't, he would tune me out, without malice, without annoyance, and without the slightest acknowledgment that I was even in the room.

And you thought this didn't happen until the teen years.

Getting into the practice of communicating with your child on his custom wavelength is excellent preparation for those teen years, when your child will treat you to typical teen behaviors alongside her autism-influenced ones. Starting now, listen to everything your child wants to tell you, including that which is not verbal. Look at him when he speaks or otherwise attempts to communicate with you, and answer him every time. (Non-response from him tells you: message undeliverable. Try a different way.) Setting up that reciprocal exchange (he hears you, you hear him) gives him confidence in the value of his message, whatever it may be and however it may be delivered. That confidence will become the motivation that moves him beyond concrete responses to spontaneous offerings, and on to initiating thoughtful and thought-filled conversation, something parents and teachers of language-challenged children alike yearn for.

While you work on framing your communication in more concrete terms, your child will give you gentle, judgment-free direction to keep you on track. It tickled our family to pieces when Bryce became able to handle answering the telephone. My mother, a health professional with ample understanding of her grandchildren's challenges, nonetheless tripped herself up nearly every time she called. "Hi Bryce," she'd say. "What are you doing?" To which he would reply, "Well, Grandma, I'm talking to you on the phone." We all learned to ask more concrete questions, the kinds that lead to conversation. What did you do in science class today? What would you like to do on Saturday? What book are you reading this week?

My most infamous idiom tale unraveled when Bryce was seven. I call it The Terrible Weary Battle of the Hangnail. You'll recognize it as one of those dreadful incidents that escalate from nothing to warfare before you have time to realize what's happening.

He came to me with a tiny hangnail on the index finger. No big deal, I said, I'll just nip it off with the nail clippers.

"Noooooooooooo!" he shrieked, with gale force. "It will HURT."

This child had spent his whole life being impervious to pain and cold. For reasons I could not imagine, this hangnail rose up as an antagonist of Goliath proportions.

First, the usual rebuttals. It won't hurt. I promise. I'll be quick. Look the other way. No? Okay, you can do it yourself. No clippers? Just bite it off. No. We'll numb it with an ice pack first. No. We'll soften it up with a warm bath. No.

Out came plans B, C, D, E, F and G, like horrid Cat in the Hat variations. All were rejected. Exasperation on both sides escalated sharply.

The evening wore on. Was that me, almost shouting? I felt myself losing it, being sucked in, towed down, unable to break the fall. Now two people were miserable instead of one.

"Look," I said. "Here are the choices: I nip it off. You nip it off. Or you live with it."

"Noooooooooooo!"

Envision the scarlet face, tears flying, and hair matted with sweat.

Bedtime came, and with it, a mom determined to spare two people a sleepless night. As I bent to tuck him in, stealthily palming the nail clipper, I grabbed his finger and the hangnail was history. An unforgettable look of pure surprise eased across his face.

"There," I said. "Did it hurt?"

"No."

The next morning I took him up on my lap and told him two things. First, he had to trust me. If I told him something would not hurt, I meant it. I would always be honest with him if something was going to hurt, like a shot. I respected his preference for the truth, however unpleasant.

Then I told him I admired his tenacity, meaning that he stood by what he believed, didn't back down, resisted pressure. That took strength and courage. "You stuck to your guns," I said, "and that can be a good thing." The words hadn't cleared my lips before I knew I had goofed.

"I don't want to stick to a gun!" he cried, alarmed.

And then:

"Are you sure you didn't mean ... gum?"

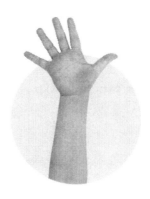

Chapter Five

Listen to all the ways
I'm trying to communicate.

"You can't rush art."

Bryce turned his bottomless blue eyes on his first-grade teacher and delivered this zinger as she hustled the class to clean up their paints: "Quick-quick-quick! It's time for music! Brushes in the sink! Line up at the door! Let's go!" Bryce had just discovered the wonder of mixing orange and green paint to make brown for his version of Van Gogh's *Sunflowers*, and he didn't appreciate the hurry-scurry. His teacher couldn't wait to repeat his remark to me because "of course, he is right."

What she didn't know was that he lifted the response wholesale (words, inflection and tempo), right out of *Toy Story 2*. Bryce had a breathtaking command of delayed echolalia. When his own limited vocabulary failed him, he had split-second retrieval of functional responses from the encyclopedic stash of movie scripts stored on the hard drive of his brain.

Echolalia is a verbal behavior common in autism wherein the child repeats chunks of language that he has heard uttered by others. Echolalia can be immediate (child echoes something that has just been said to or near him), delayed (child repeats something he's heard in recent, mid- or distant past) or perseverative (child repeats the same phrase or question over and over again). For many parents (count me as one), echolalia incites a piercing sense of panic that foments when exchanges of fact, feeling, and thought cannot flow freely among ourselves, our child, and the rest of the world.

At the time of the can't-rush-art incident, ninety percent of Bryce's speech was delayed echolalia. He employed it so skillfully that it was largely undetectable to anyone but our family. Still, I was desperate to squash it—a common, understandable but misguided desire for parents in my position. Because the speech isn't spontaneous, it can seem like (since we're quoting movies) "what we've got here is failure to communicate." (*Cool Hand Luke,* 1967) Echolalic speech often doesn't seem to have any relevance to what's happening at the moment, although to the child, it does. He may be three or four associative links ahead of you, making it your tricky but necessary job to discover the correlation.

Echolalia is only one aspect of language development, albeit one that generates considerable emotion in parents. We want it gone. I have felt with a mother's heart, as you may be feeling, the urgency to have my child produce "normal" language, the kind that erases some of the stark difference between him and his age peers. In that urgency, we must not lose sight of the fact that while he has yet to develop basic vocabulary and the skills involved with generative speech, he still needs a way to communicate his needs, fears, and wants. If you take away only one thing from this chapter, let it be this: having a means of functional communication, whatever it may be, is essential to any child, but more so to the child with autism. If your child cannot get her needs met and fears quelled, her world and yours can be a horrid place. Without functional communication expect to see her frustration and fear play out in behavior, as she tries to let you know by the only means available to her that things are not as they should be for her. Once she is comfortable that she can communicate regardless of where she is between calm and calamity, and that you will listen and hear her regardless of her mode of communication, she can begin to build an understanding of all facets of communication, including the ones that go beyond mere vocabulary.

The typical early words and petite first sentences of childhood seem so simple on the surface. You want your child to say "mama" and "doggie," then "I want juice" and "Can I play?" and "I love you." But oh, how much is going on in those simple phrases. Speech (the physical ability to produce vocal sounds) is only the beginning component of language (putting words together in a way that conveys meaning to others). Language alone doesn't create conversation (establishing social contact with others using verbal and nonverbal communication). As a baby, your child made his needs and moods known in nonverbal ways. Most children progress to uttering words, then stringing those words together into phrases and sentences. As they grow, their language becomes much more than a tool for slapping labels on items, feelings, and actions. It becomes a means to express their thoughts and emotions, and to interact with others socially. The social use of language, called *pragmatics*, is the synergistic brew of words, gestures, facial expressions, and social understanding we use, often unconsciously or instinctively, to communicate with each other. At any one or many points along this developmental timeline, autism can hinder your child's understanding of how these tools work to connect us or to separate us. In Chapter Eight, we'll further explore the social aspects of conversation, the everything-else beyond our words that helps us relate to others.

I can never forget how Bryce's early struggles with speech challenged his efforts to socialize, impacted his emotional health, and obscured his cognitive capabilities. Fortunately, two things happened concurrently that eased my mind enough that I could back off and let him work through his echolalia in his own way and at his own pace. First, I read an article by a young man with autism, twenty years old, successfully making his way through a four-year college. He described how he still employed echolalia in his everyday social communication, and that he alone knew it. I thought, *Huh. Maybe the stress I'm reaping on this issue isn't warranted.*

I called in our district autism specialist. She offered wise and memorable advice: "I know you want to stamp this out. But don't. Don't try to go around, go through it. I promise you it will not last forever, but give him the time he needs to work through it."

Though I didn't know the word for it at the time, Bryce was a gestalt learner. *Gestalt* is a German word that means whole or complete. Gestalt learners take experiences as one piece, without being able to see the individual components. Many children with autism learn language in this manner, absorbing it in chunks, rather than as individual words. As opposed to gestalt, we call word-by-word learning *analytic*. It may seem as though analytic language learners are more typical in the population than gestalt learners. In fact many children with autism, particularly Asperger's, are analytic learners who can easily associate meaning with individual words. Both analytic and gestalt are legitimate ("normal") learning styles.

A speech therapist can guide your child through echolalia and other parts of language and communication development, including the process of learning to break apart "gestalts" and reconstruct the smaller pieces into spontaneous speech. As you embark upon therapy, remember that each child will have a unique response pattern. There's no correct timetable, and sometimes progress may look like regression. If your child spouts lengthy, eloquent scripts, his learning to generate simple sentences of his own may temporarily sound toddler-esque. It's not. It's healthy language development.

In the meantime, it may ease your anxiety about your child's echolalia if you take time to notice how he uses it. Chances are he isn't just playing files in his head; he's using it as a means of communication that makes sense to him. His echolalia may be functional and interactive in a number of ways. Listen and note. See if he might use it to:

- Reciprocate conversation, respond where he knows an exchange is expected.
- Ask for or request something, either an object or someone's attention.
- Offer information or opinion.
- Protest or deny the actions or requests of others.
- Give instructions or directives.
- Put a name or a label to an item, activity or place.

As a fourth-grader, Bryce sat for the usual round of triennial standardized testing, the results of which decreed his vocabulary to be severely subpar. This stunned me. Coming from three-word phrases at age four and ninety percent echolalic speech at age six, I marveled at his accomplishments with the spoken word by age ten, which included speaking with ease in front of groups. I asked to see the test material. Among other things, he had "incorrectly identified" the words cactus and violin. This brought my hackles up. Those words represented things that he seldom, if ever, encountered in his daily life, his reading, or his movie viewing. And he had gotten the context correct, identifying the cactus as a "desert plant" and the violin as a "music player." The rigidity of the testing infuriated me, but it did make me realize how, in listening to and responding to him, I automatically decoded the irregular language in both his spontaneous and echolalic speech. I didn't want to spend my conversational time with him correcting grammar and syntax, so I did the translation in my head and continued to exchange thoughts with him uninterrupted.

In one sense, I was doing the right thing, validating his means of functional communication and with it, his self-image. But I took the test results as a wake-up call that I needed to do more everyday feeding in of language as well as checking for comprehension in both the spoken and written word. For instance, we came across this passage in a story: "He ripped the handbag from her grasp." Bryce looked blank, so we stopped and I went over the words rip, grasp, and handbag. "Oh," he said, exasperated. "He stole her purse. Why doesn't it just say that? 'He stole her purse?'" This led to a discussion of how words, like colors, come in many "shades" and how varying our words can make a story colorful. We had a good time coming up with a long and comical list of ways to say big: large, huge, gigantic, immense, enormous, whopping, humongous, colossal, and on and on. It was a light bulb moment for both of us. He hadn't thought of words that way, and I hadn't thought of offering them so.

This reinforced one of the first and most elemental pieces of advice Bryce's speech therapist had given us: that we work hard to maintain a language-rich environment around him. A child not frequently exposed to other speaking people will develop language much more slowly. In particular, if your child is in a self-contained special education classroom, she may not have much exposure to typically-developing kidspeak. Alongside using visual supports for our kids with emerging speech (we delve into that in Chapter Six), we must surround them with words and language. Talk out the thoughts in your head, verbalize what you are doing and why. Look at your child when you speak to him, and answer him every time he speaks to you or otherwise attempts to communicate, letting him know you value everything he has to say, regardless of whether you understand him. Read to him, tell him stories, sing to him. Singing is speech, so if your child learns songs easily, use that strength to enhance his language skills. Talk about any new words in the song he may not understand. Distinguish nonsense words from real words.

Putting your child on the spot to respond in words or engage in conversation can be very stressful for him, so help ease that performance anxiety by putting manageable parameters on verbal exchanges. Try this two-minute/two-minute rule: tell him you'd like to hear about his day at school, his favorite toy or book, the dog, or any subject that interests him. If he's willing, give him two minutes to gather his thoughts, then watch, listen and respond to him for two minutes. In family conversation, learn to pause for responses. Many families chat and banter at a rapid-fire pace that leaves the child with autism unable to keep up. To slow the overall pace of exchanges and give your child a better chance to participate, wait a few seconds before responding.

"Use your words." As you push your child or student toward verbal communication, how many times have your prompted him to do this, and with how many different inflections? One day encouraging, gently coaxing. The next day stern, with a shot of frustration. Another day, weary and pleading. All the words your child has may not be enough to make his needs, wants, thoughts, and ideas known. She may have learned a word, but producing it requires added layers of processing and skill. Articulating her thoughts and feelings may be easy one day, impossible the next when sensory issues amplify and interfere, or when your expectation that she maintain certain behaviors depletes all the energy she can muster. Think you know how it feels to be forced to multi-task under pressure? Your child or student's list includes trying to self-regulate multiple hyper- or hypoactive senses simultaneously, intercept and interpret visual and auditory clues and cues floating around, employ and act upon appropriate social thinking, and then produce language as well. "Use your words" is a worthy goal, as speech is the ultimate portable, standalone, all-terrain, all-hours, all-weather communication device. But on the way to achieving any degree of that goal, it is compulsory that we acknowledge *all* our child or student's attempts to communicate, in whatever form the message comes.

And after investing so much heartfelt effort in helping our children find their words, you may find that a great irony of the twenty-first century sneaks in to ambush you. Without ongoing attention, that language-rich environment can slip away, disappearing into the crevices of technology and changing culture. Even when our kids do achieve the ability to speak, reciprocal speech, of any duration, may be a hard-won learned skill. The essential component of any learned skill is practice, practice, and more practice. And that is why a sad realization came to me during an ordinary morning round of errands, one poignant and worrisome reason why reciprocal speech remains a challenge for our kids: we no longer talk to the people in our immediate community. My morning was a potent example. I got cash from an ATM; I didn't talk to a bank teller. I scanned my groceries through the self-checkout line; I didn't talk to a checker. Our library has automated checkout; I didn't talk to the librarian. I mailed a package at the Automated Postal Center without talking to a clerk. I'd bypassed at least half a dozen of what, not so long ago, would have been opportunities for human interaction. *Wall Street Journal* publisher Les Hinton has been quoted as saying that the scarcest resource of the twenty-first century, "after water and food and all of that," will be human attention.

A language-rich environment? More like a language-depleted landscape.

Automation, electronic communication and social media have a legitimate, immutable place in our culture. But if we value the stimulation, joy, and functionality of reciprocal speech—conversation—we must teach our children, by example, to come out from behind their computer and phone screens and practice *talking* to others. Our speech therapist's advice about creating a language-rich environment came at a time when the use of language hadn't yet been appropriated by electronics, when being conversational included vocal inflections, facial expression, and body language. You know, like Skype without the screen. Of the many parent-teen conflicts my husband and I expected to face, we never dreamed we'd be considered counter-culture because we wanted our children to *speak* to other humans.

Sooner or later, our kids will have to talk to the people in their community because some relationships cannot be relegated to a screen—the doctor, the dentist, the bus driver, the hair stylist, the flight attendant, the policeman, the firefighter, the clergy, the lifeguard, the piano teacher, the coach, the lawyer, the judge. It will happen if we help our children expand their communication skills by respecting their current abilities, and providing a variety of means to convey wants, needs, thoughts, feelings, and ideas under all circumstances. We've then opened a door to a place where they can experience conversation as camaraderie rather than combat, to a place where genuine communication connects us all.

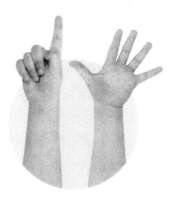

Chapter Six

Picture this!
I am visually oriented.

One of my favorite spunky girls is *My Fair Lady's* Eliza Doolittle, a character created as a walking, breathing language experiment. She makes herself impossible to ignore in a number of ways, never more so than in the song "Show Me," when she admonishes her lover to knock it off with the "Words, words, words! I'm so sick of words!" followed by, "Don't waste my time, show me!"

Many children with autism would cheer her sentiments.

Visual cuing is hardly a novelty. If you carry a day-planner (electronic or paper) or keep a calendar on your desk or wall, you're using a visual support. Sign language—I've seen it called handspeak—is a highly developed form of visual communication that includes facial expression and body language in a manner similar to how vocal volume and inflection enhance the meaning of spoken language. Semaphore uses flag signals rather than words and letters to communicate visually across distances. Go to a baseball game and watch the third base coach rub his forearm, grab his belt and slap his chest. He's not auditioning for a Jane Goodall film. He's telling his base runner to stay put unless the ball is a hopper to shallow right field. All these modes of interface use something other than spoken words to achieve functional communication.

Your child or student may have a profound need for visual cuing. Many individuals with autism think in images, not words. Their primary language is pictorial, not verbal. A child may have minimal verbal expressive language but are we arrogant enough, or naïve enough, to think that this means he has no thoughts, preferences, opinions, ideas, or beliefs? Does that tree falling in the woods make no sound because no one is around to hear it? Nonsense. Your child or student may be translating his life experiences into pictures in his head. It is a language no less legitimate than the one you use to speak, and it's the one you must accommodate if you want to reach and teach him in a meaningful way that leads to meaningful results.

Temple Grandin elevated the world's awareness of her visual orientation in her 1996 book *Thinking in Pictures*, which opens:

> "I think in pictures. Words are like a second language to me. I translate both spoken and written words into full-color movies, complete with sound, which run like a VCR tape in my head. When somebody speaks to me, his words are instantly translated into pictures. Language-based thinkers often find this phenomenon difficult to understand."

As we established in Chapter Five, the ability to communicate, to receive, express and feel heard, is fundamental to the overall healthy functioning of your child, of any person. Without an effective means of communication, a visually oriented child (square peg) continually being squeezed into a verbally oriented world (round hole) is bound to feel unheard, embattled, overwhelmed, and outnumbered. What should she do, but retreat?

Creating a visual schedule or other visual strategy to help your child navigate his school day or home routine may be one of the first tools suggested by your school team or by your own research. Why? It:

- Provides the structure and predictability essential to children with autism. Knowing what happens next frees her to focus on the task or activity at hand without the anxiety of worrying about what comes next and when.

- Provides a touchstone, a consistent source of information that enables her to trust that events will unfold logically and she can feel safe in that routine.

- Reinforces the first/then strategy for dealing with less enjoyable tasks. "First you finish eight math problems, then you may have five minutes on the computer" helps him feel motivated rather than lapsing into avoidance or procrastination.

- Increases his ability to perform tasks autonomously and to transition between activities independently.

- Can help ease the rigidity of thinking and inflexibility that frequently characterize autism. As the child's confidence in his independence grows, you can insert curveballs into the schedule in the form of varied activities, or a question mark, indicating a surprise activity.

- Can incorporate social skill-building. The schedule might include a five-minute "play [or read] with a classmate" time or "say or wave goodbye to three people."

All of this builds and fortifies your child or student's ability to understand and meet the expectations of those around him.

Not all visual schedules are created equal any more than all calendars are. The common element is their sequential nature. Beyond that, the size, style of representation, portability, and length vary infinitely.

We employed Bryce's first visual schedule when he entered Pre-K, long before the convenience and flexibility of handheld electronic devices. We used Boardmasters, a system of simple line drawings depicting various activities, to create small laminated squares with Velcro on the back that we arranged in a strip depicting the day's routine: get up, eat breakfast, get dressed, brush teeth, get on bus. Bryce did each task, then removed the picture, dropped it in an attached envelope and moved on to the next thing. It worked, sort of, but he never seemed engaged in it. A year later, we discovered that Bryce didn't relate to artwork. Stick figures had little meaning for him, nor did he want anything to do with fanciful or abstract illustration. He liked concrete images—photographs. He became much more engaged when I presented stories or instructions with photographs.

Whether electronic, paper, or other medium, the first step in setting up a successful visual communication strategy is to identify your child or student's *level of representation*. That's fancy talk for determining what is visually meaningful to him. Bryce required photographs; for another child, it might be stick figures, pencil drawings or full-color art. More concrete-thinking children may need to begin at the very basic level of the physical object. As the child grows older, it might be words in combination with pictures, and perhaps someday, words alone (then it gets called a to-do list). This attention to modification as the child ages is a key element of the effectiveness of visual supports, ensuring that they continue to be useful in a manner that doesn't invite ridicule or ostracism. Consider as well how your child best tracks information. Don't assume it's left to right. It may be top to bottom. An occupational therapist can help you determine this. How many increments should appear on a schedule or a page at one time? Don't overwhelm. Start with two or three and work up from there.

Visual strategies are not something to phase out as your child becomes progressively more independent. They are life-long tools that foster organization, time management, flexibility, initiative, and a host of other executive functioning skills necessary for self-sufficiency. Over time, I keep coming up against gentle reminders that a visual schedule is more than a strip of stick-figure sketches that we used to help Bryce learn to get ready for preschool. The level of representation and sophistication may escalate with the years, but not the need, and not the stability it provides and the stress it relieves. It's what keeps the calendar printers and smart phone designers in business.

In the first weeks of middle school, in a new building full of new teachers and a sea of new faces, Bryce faced a formidable challenge. Outdoor School is a popular long-standing program in our county wherein sixth graders go to local camps for a week to learn about native ecosystems. It's a terrific program, but one that raised many questions on both my part and Bryce's. He had never spent five nights away from home without family. He would be under the supervision of two teachers who had known him less than six weeks, and the rest of the camp staff, who didn't know him at all. He would have to tolerate unfamiliar routine, unpredictable weather, sleeping and eating with children he had never met before, and perhaps worst of all—camp food.

Although both school and camp staff assured me they would make any accommodation necessary, Bryce wasn't sure he wanted to go, changing his mind from hour to hour. We drove up to the camp for visitation, through which he remained silent. He surveyed the dining room, which would be, he was sure, a source of suffering. But wait—a spark of interest! On the wall by the door, larger than life, hung the daily schedule: 6:45 wake up, 7:15 flag, 7:30 breakfast, 10:30 wildlife studies, 11:15 lunch, 12:00 quiet time, 5:00 dinner, 5:45 songs, 6:30 campfire and class meeting, etc. The whole day, mapped out in manageable increments.

"Would somebody get me a copy of this?" he asked.

The staff not only shrunk the schedule to palm size, they laminated it, punched a hole in the corner and hung it around his neck on a lanyard. Before he left he also asked me for the meal-by-meal schedule I had gotten from the head cook, so he would know exactly when he would eat camp food and when he would ask for one his own meals that I sent up with him.

Bryce's teacher reported that, armed with his two frequently consulted visual schedules, he had easily settled in. The visual schedules provided predictability and a concrete routine that made the exotic, intimidating setting not only manageable but enjoyable. Bryce organized and directed his cabin's skit, a spoof on the morning inspection routine. At the final campfire, he moved his teacher to tears as he spoke about feeling unsure when he arrived but making new friends throughout the week. He wore the same pair of socks the entire week and ignored the other five pairs in his bag. He had a typical Outdoor School experience and he spent the rest of the year telling anyone who asked that it was the best part of sixth grade.

For teaching to be effective, you must be heard, and many children with autism hear better with a picture. Also recognize that what happens between the words and the picture is translation. You may need to slow down your usual pace of communication to allow that processing to happen. Give her extra time to respond, don't repeat the same instructions over and over if they're not getting through. "Please don't 'expline!'" Eliza Doolittle scolds. "Show me!"

The success your child achieves with the aid of his visual supports may leave you sighing in relief and satisfaction, thinking "I don't know what we'd do without them." That's your cue to take steps to ensure you never have to find out. You need backup or contingency plans and tools, because electronic devices glitch, mysteriously lose files, run out of power at the worst possible moments, get lost or stolen, go through the laundry or that irresistible sprinkler, fall into the bathtub or toilet. Non-electronic supports are no less subject to physical damage or loss. Having a Plan B at the ready when the child's primary support fails is as important as having the supports in the first place. I'm cautious myself in this regard, keeping both electronic and paper calendars, knowing that there will be at least several times a year when, for purposes of por-tability (iPads in the pouring rain at Outdoor School wouldn't have been an option), cross-reference, or where-the-heck-did-I-leave-that-dang-phone?, I'll be glad I did.

For many children with autism, visuals make sense where oral or written words don't. Picture it (get it?) this way: visual images are the powerful medium that organizes and explains your child's world, tames its stress, gives him understandable guidance and boundaries. See it his way; teach him in a way that makes sense to him. Life then becomes less of a battle and he need be less of a warrior. He comes, he sees—he conquers.

Chapter Seven

Focus and build on what I can do rather than what I can't do.

When my brother first read *Ten Things* he commented, "Number seven is true for all kids." He's right, and I would extend it to all people, not just kids.

Yet many families and educators unwittingly tumble into the Swamp of Unmet Expectations. This is where a child's potential goes to die if we as adults fail to detach our personal aspirations from those appropriate for our child.

Adapted PE teacher Sarah Spella sees it all the time. "Parents get into a grieving process," she says. "Their child isn't going to be a certain way that they expected her to be, and their attitude becomes a huge handicap for the child. I see many cases where the parent may be very much into physical fitness and sports. Their too-high expectations in that area can turn the child completely off to the very things the parent wants him to be. I work with these children every week, and they don't care a hoot for PE." They may have skills on par with their typically developing peers, she explains, but they process those skills differently, and it all means nothing without a belief system behind it. "I can tell them for years, I know you can do this. But if they don't have that full parental support, there is only so much I can do in thirty minutes a week."

The distinction between what constitutes a disability and what constitutes a different ability is much more than pretentious political correctness. We are all differently abled. As George Carlin put it, "Barry Bonds can't play the cello and Yo Yo Ma can't hit the curveball." My husband can't write books and I can't engineer industrial air-flow systems. It never comes up for discussion; we're happy knowing that our different skills and abilities mean we each have a constructive place in the world.

I've read my share of sad emails and stories that echo the can't-do lament of parents, but nevertheless have potential for happy endings. "Four generations of Andersons have played the violin, and I can't even get him to look at one." No kidding. Is there a musical instrument more sensory-hellish than a violin? Imagine the screechy sound a new learner produces, the strings that bite into tender fingers and the sensation of having a weirdly shaped vibrating box parked under your sweaty chin while you hold both arms up at unnatural angles. It took someone outside this family to notice that the child, while not inclined to the violin, was a natural on the golf course, with an easy and accurate swing. I hope the family took the opportunity not only to learn something new from their child but also to validate his capability.

Another family, passionate skiers, gloomily accepted that their child's vestibular issues made skiing and snowboarding abhorrent to him. While at the beach one summer, Mom noticed her son could spend hours moving piles of sand around, examining them from every angle, making structural adjustments. That winter she bought him a set of snow block molds (plain plastic boxes) and away he went building igloos, forts, and castles. Her discovery of what he could do rather than what he couldn't do meant that the family could still spend a day together on the mountain, with each family member rotating "Andy time" with the snow forts while the others skied. Eventually, Andy acclimated to the snow enough to try gentle inner-tubing and snow-shoeing. Someday I may see him up there on Nordic skis.

Being able to focus and build on the can-do rather than can't-do of your child is all about perspective. Earlier in the book we talked about reframing your child's challenging behaviors as positives. It bears repeating. Is the child standoffish, or able to work independently? Is he reckless, or adventuresome and willing to try new experiences? Is he obsessively neat, or does he have outstanding organizational skills? Do you hear nonstop pestering with questions, or do you see curiosity, tenacity, and persistence? Later in the book, we'll talk more about how the perspective you hold about your child and his abilities now will directly affect his ability to grow into self-sufficient adulthood. For now, I ask:

Can you do this? Can you shift perspective, build upon all that is positive in your child?

Will you do this?

My father marveled that he had "never, ever known a happier baby" than Bryce, adding, "and I've been around a lot of babies." I agreed. Bryce, a sweet and placid infant, went everywhere with me.

We enrolled him in a preschool program two mornings a week when he was two. September wasn't yet over before the teacher reported that Bryce played in a corner by himself, that his language skills were underdeveloped, that he didn't participate in table activities and that he hit and pushed his classmates. I struggled to believe this because it was so out of character. By spring conference time, nothing had changed. "Bryce usually plays by himself," stated the written report. "He's quiet and will observe other children. He has a hard time following directions. Bryce doesn't like art projects or table activities. He says words but we have a hard time understanding him. He imitates the other children. Bryce has a short attention span. He doesn't interact during circle time."

Wow, I thought. *That's a damn lot of can'ts. He's* two.

The recitation of can't/doesn't carried into the next year. At November parent conferences, I politely interrupted the teacher to ask if we could refocus on things that Bryce could and did do. With this prompt, I heard how he entertained himself for long periods, loved physical play whether indoors or out, sought out sand table play, and had a gift for imitation. We concluded that his language delays interfered substantially with his ability to become a part of the classroom community. I thought, *here is something I could do*, and we entered the world of private speech therapy. Soon, he was putting together intelligible three-word phrases at school.

Still, my asking for cans and enlisting professional help didn't improve the big picture. The winter report came, by now wearyingly familiar: wants to interact with other children but doesn't know how, sits for long periods playing by himself, has a hard time listening in a group situation. I felt the time had come to stop the spinning. I asked for a meeting with the teachers and the school principal. After listening yet again to the same can'ts, a touchy exchange unfolded in which I asked the teacher flat out if maybe she didn't like Bryce. She reacted as if she'd been shot. I instantly felt crummy-and-a-half, wondering if I had poisoned the productivity out of the meeting. "No, it's a legitimate question," said the principal. "You had to ask." The answer was that Bryce's teachers loved him, but his needs were beyond their ability to handle within the resources of the school. The meeting ended with the principal's decision to refer him to public Early Intervention services.

"What is that?" I asked, having never heard the term "early intervention." What was happening?

"They are people who will help," she said. And the Early Intervention teachers and therapists were remarkable can-do people. They continually told me how "cool" Bryce was (and why), how far they thought he could go, and how we could chart the journey to get there. They focused on his strengths and on teaching tactics and physical accommodations to ameliorate his challenges. It resonated with us all, Bryce included.

The earliest books I read on the subject of autism told a different story, one fraught with dismal assumptions. He won't form relationships, won't get married, won't be able to hold a job, won't understand the nuances of the law or the banking system or the bus system. Won't, won't, won't—yet more extensions of "can't." Splayed on the page in black and white, more nay-saying, written by people who supposedly knew more than I did. *I am not*, I told myself, *in denial*. And already, deep in the space between the gray matter and the heart, a tiny voice strained to be heard. *Don't believe it. It isn't true unless you let it be.* I had just started out but I was already done listening to the nay-sayers and their choruses of can't.

One of the most important things you can do as a parent is to heed the strong inner voice that tells you what is right for your child. No one else loves her as you do and no one else is as invested in her future. The most popular treatments and thinking of the day may be right for many children but may not be for yours. One particular approach to autism was prevalent in the early 1990s. I read about it, loathed it, knew with 200% certainty that it wouldn't work with Bryce, and during a memorable school meeting, told those can-do early intervention people: "Do this to my kid and I will kill you." Happily for me, they had already decided the same thing (the teacher later told me she wanted to stand up and applaud). Most of them are still in my life, now cherished friends, and boy, do they remember that conversation. It gets revisited on a regular basis.

I realize you may find the preceding paragraph provocative. Since writing the first edition of this book I'm asked regularly, sometimes nastily, to reveal the approach I so loathed. My answer is always the same. I'm not going to tell you what it was, because if you ask the question, you missed the point. The take-away of my story is that you educate yourself about resources available and pursue only those that make sense for your child.

My can-do attitude about Bryce grew strong in the face of my early confrontations with can't-do. That's not to say the can't-do messages I received about him didn't scare me; of course they scared me. They also challenged me, made me mad, made me think, *Oh yeah? We'll see about that.*

If you haven't been in the habit of conscientiously focusing on what your child can do, how do you start? First, acknowledge that this is a shift in mindset, and it will take time and practice. Next, look for an indication of your child's learning style.

"Do not ask how smart is my child, but how is my child smart?" counsels David Sousa, author of *How the Brain Learns*. Typically developing children may learn in a variety of ways. Children with autism may favor one learning style almost to exclusion of others.

Sequential learners benefit from step-by-step instructions, are frequently good at rote memorization, may be called neat freaks (a phrase that needs to go) because they like visual organization. Gestalt or global learners assimilate information in chunks, sizing up the big picture first, then chunking it down into details. Naturalist learners learn best in natural settings among naturally-occurring elements. They like to interact with animals and outdoor surroundings and may demonstrate an unusual ability to categorize, organize, or preserve information. Call it advanced sorting skills. Kinesthetic learners learn by doing, seeking to experience the world through large and small movement of their bodies. They are climbers, runners, dancers, actors; they enjoy crafts and tools. The spatial learner is your little construction worker or chess player. He likes to plan and/or build and draw things he sees in his head, and he relates well to maps, puzzles, charts, and graphs. He seems to have an inborn understanding of concepts of physics and geometry, but may be poor at spelling and memorizing verbal passages. Many children with autism who are hypersensitive to noise and have delayed verbal skills may be musical learners. They perceive patterns in sound (rhythms, rhymes, raps), hold melodies in their head, and compose their own tunes as mnemonic devices.

Understanding how your child or student processes information opens the floodgates to learning. You'll be able to guide her to success in activities inside and outside of school through which she can experience the self-confidence necessary to confront tasks or events that challenge her. You'll be more flexible and enthusiastic in your approach, and you'll see it in the increased enthusiasm she will have for learning because finally, it makes some sense to her.

In doing so, you must throw out conventional or typical growth charts and timelines that you may see in books or doctors' offices. Much of it is irrelevant to your child. At the outset of my journey, I learned that one of the hallmarks of autism is uneven development. One of Bryce's early friends was a four-year-old oceanography wiz who had forgotten more about coral reef habitats and bioluminescence than I will ever know. His mother told me she would trade it all for a few moments of eye contact and a smile like Bryce's. I hope that by now she's gotten both.

Bryce does have a brilliant smile, but the conventional timelines have been meaningless for him in many ways. He didn't talk reliably until age four, and didn't read reliably until the fourth grade. He loved swimming pools but clung to the sides, a blond barnacle, steadfastly refusing swim lessons until age eight when, with the right teacher and the right pool, he churned through all six levels of the swim program in just a few months. His instructors told us that most kids get stuck at a certain level, sometimes for months, before moving on. As he did with his language development, Bryce learned to swim in a gestalt manner—big, albeit delayed, chunks rather than the more typical progression of little steps.

And now a word about our responsibilities and vulnerabilities as parents, family members, and teachers in can-do vs. can't-do. One of the most distressing Internet posts I ever read popped up on a site whose members were having a spirited discussion about my Ten Things. One mom, who admitted to feeling "tired and snarky," wrapped up a long I-love-you-but message to her child with this: "Oh, and God, if you're listening, I take back what I stupidly vowed when she was small and adorable and didn't hit me, about not wanting her any other way than what she was. I'll take that trade-in now, for the kid she was supposed to be."

I wanted to both weep and rage when I read this because I am beyond certain that her child hasn't asked God if she can trade in her mother for the parent she was supposed to be. I weep for the everyday magic this mom will miss in her child, the opportunities and accomplishments drowned in the stew of bitterness. I rage at the no-win situation in which she's placed her child, the unfairness of blaming autism for even the regular-kid things she does: "Don't feed almonds and Barbie parts to the dog. I don't appreciate the extra mess."

Though I empathized with this mother's soul-crushing fatigue, and though most of her post was snarly, I could still pick out building blocks of hope that had the power to turn the whole thing around. She worried for the future of her child as an adult and she wanted to lessen the impact of her child's autism on the siblings. She engaged her child in occupational and speech therapies (albeit referred to as "tortures"); she weighed the pros and cons of medications. So while her harsh words made me cringe, I can hope she found her way to building on what both she and her child can do.

If you're treading quicksand in the swamp of what-might-have-been, you can be sure that's the message your child gets. You're a rare person if being constantly reminded of your shortcomings spurs you to improve. For the rest of us, it's a self-esteem squasher. Time to grab for that overhead vine and realize that only a pencil dot separates "bitter" and "better."

As parents (and family members and teachers), we do need to reflect this advice about can-do and can't-do back on ourselves. When a diagnosis of autism comes in, many parents feel overwhelming urgency. They rush to read everything about autism they can get their hands on, join online discussion groups and network like mad with other parents. Sometimes the ensuing crush of information overwhelms. Some of it is encouraging and uplifting; some of it is depressing and spirit-sapping. There are professionals to consult, school and therapy programs to be put into action, medications and special diets to consider, and worries about how to pay for it. If you allow this avalanche of new information to overtake you, you risk overdosing on the very tools that are going to get you through the long haul ahead. Paralysis sets in. It's real; it happens.

Here is one thing you can do. Adjust yourself to this new challenge at a measured, reasonable pace by knowing this:

You have time. You have lots of time.

You have today.

You have tomorrow.

You have next week.

You have next month and next year, and many years after that.

Every passing year brings new information and understanding, for you, and for the fields of medicine and education.

Tune out the naysayers. Stay the course. Results will come.

Chapter Eight

Help me with social interactions.

We can be blunt with each other here. Kids with autism or Asperger's frequently stand out as social oddballs. The heartbreak it causes, to the child and to the parent, stirs in many parents an intense need to fix that facet of their child. If social competence was a physiological function, we could throw medication, nutrition, exercise, or physical therapy at it and make it happen. If kids with autism were curious, outgoing, motivated learners, we could cultivate social intelligence curriculum-style.

Too often, our kids aren't like that, and social awareness isn't a set of concrete, itemized skills. Basic manners (please and thank you, use tissue, not sleeve, wait your turn) can and should be taught, regardless of the child's level of function, but learning to be at ease among others in the bustle and nuances of daily life is infinitely more complex. Social skills (behaviors we want our child to exhibit) are the end product of an intricate organism of developmental elements we call "social thinking."

Just as we all have to learn to walk before we run, we must teach our children to "think social" before they can act social, with understanding and positive intent, not just by rote repetition or in fear of consequences. Social thinking presents your child with the challenge of factoring context and perspective into his actions—to consider the physical, social, and temporal aspects of his surroundings, to take into account the thoughts and viewpoints of others, to use shared imagination to connect with a play partner, and to comprehend that others have favorable or not-so-favorable thoughts and reactions to him based on what he says and does. Social thinking is the source from which our social behaviors spring, and this social-emotional intelligence may be a bigger determinant in a child's long-term success in life than cognitive intelligence.

Parent or teacher, home or school, teaching a child with autism to think social begins with chucking any assumptions you may harbor about his ability to absorb social sensibility by simply being around and observing socially adept people, or that he will somehow, someday outgrow his social cluelessness. To date, our education system has based curriculum standards on the flawed supposition that all children enter the world with an intact social processing brain and on a presumed social developmental progression. It makes no sense (and is grossly unfair to the child) to respond to a child's social snafus based on such assumptions and then blame his autism when our attempts to teach don't register with him. What our children need is for us to shift perspective and start building their social awareness at its roots.

When we say we want our child to learn social skills, we're really reaching for something grander. We want him to be able to fit into the world around him, to function independently at school, in the community, at work, and within his personal relationships. Bryce stated this goal from early adolescence and, he told me, it had always been his goal, long before he could articulate it or even put a name to it in his childhood thoughts. More than playing by a rule book, being social is a state of confident being that grows with careful nurturing of social thinking skills, starting when a child is very young:

- Perspective taking: being able to see and experience the world from standpoints other than your own, and to see these different perspectives as opportunities to learn and grow.
- Flexibility: being able to roll with unforeseen changes in routine and expectation, being able to recognize that mistakes are not an end result but a part of learning and growing, and that disappointments are matters of degree.
- Curiosity: drawing motivation from thinking about the "why" behind things—why something exists, why its existence is important, why others feel the way they do, and how it reflects back and matters to us.
- Self-esteem: believing enough in your own abilities to risk trying new things, having enough respect and affection for yourself to be able to deflect the cruel and thoughtless remarks and actions of others as saying more about them than you.
- Big picture thinking: appreciating that social thinking and social awareness are part of all we do, whether or not we are interacting with others. We read stories, trying to figure out the motives of characters and predict what they will do next. We

replay situations in our head, deciding whether or not we acted appropriately. Your child may tell you, "I don't care about being social; I'm happy by myself." He may mean it in the moment, and many people do generally prefer solitude to socializing. But it's also true that some of our kids adopt the I-don't-care attitude to deflect the pain of caring very much and not having the knowledge, skills, and support to overcome their social barriers, and in doing so, be able to achieve their goals and dreams in life.

- Communication: understanding that we communicate even when we are not talking. Michelle Garcia Winner (Thinking About YOU Thinking About Me, 2nd edition, 2007), who coined the term "Social Thinking" and is considered today to be one of the leading voices in the field, outlines four steps of communication that unfold in linear sequence, within milliseconds, and often without conscious thought:

  - We think about other people's thoughts and feelings as well as our own
  - We establish physical presence so people understand our intention to communicate
  - We use our eyes to monitor how people are feeling, acting, and reacting to what is happening between us
  - We use language to relate to others

Did you notice that language enters the communication equation only as the last step? And yet it's where, as parents and teachers, we typically place emphasis. Teaching only step four in the absence of the other three leaves your child or student inadequately equipped, vulnerable, and wide open to the likelihood that she will be less effective, less successful in her social communication. It's equally important to imbue your child with a sense of the role nonverbal communication plays in his social encounters. The junctures at which the subtleties of social interaction can go awry fall into three broad categories:

- Vocalic communication: He doesn't understand the myriad nuances of spoken language. He doesn't understand sarcasm, puns, idioms, metaphors, hints, slang, double entendres, hyperbole, or abstraction. He may speak in a monotone (suggesting boredom to the listener), or he may speak too loudly, too softly, too quickly, or too slowly.
- Kinesthetic communication: He doesn't understand body language, facial expressions, or emotional responses (crying, recoiling). He may use gestures or postures inappropriately and may refuse eye contact.
- Proxemic communication: He doesn't understand physical space communication, the subtle territorial cues and norms of personal boundaries. He may be an unwitting "space invader." The rules of proxemics not only vary from culture to culture, but from person to person depending upon relationship. Intimate? Casual but personal? Social only? Public space? For many kids with autism or Asperger's, deciphering proxemics requires an impossible level of inference.

There's no short cut, magic bullet, or eureka cure to your child's becoming comfortable with social interaction. It takes practice, in-the-moment, get-messy, make-mistakes practice (emphasizing that "mistake" is just another word for "practice.") Unlike the idea that providing a language-rich environment will encourage language development, mainstreaming a child with her typically-developing peers will not bring forth social thinking skills without direct, concrete teaching of social concepts. Without this direct teaching, your child will still bob along into adulthood in that same sea of social miscommunication. Teaching your child to think social and be social is a mosaic of thousands upon thousands of petite learning opportunities and encounters that, properly channeled, will coalesce into a core of self-confidence. It requires you, as his parent, his teacher, his guide, to be socially aware 110% of the time, break down the web of social intricacies, and clue him in to the social nuances that are so difficult for him to perceive.

Social navigation is necessary at every turn in our lives: at home, at work, at school, in our travels about the community, in our shopping, recreation, and worship. As you shepherd your child through this challenging landscape, I implore you to do it without the mindset that he is "less than." Sending the child a constant message that he is inherently deficient will surely build the wall that prevents the progress we want. Self-esteem, that essential component of social functioning, will not flourish in an environment that sends the message that she's not good enough the way she is. Some of her behaviors may not be conducive to her social development, but always separate the behavior from the whole child.

With Bryce, I knew from the start that we were in for a long, long trek. On a good day, it meant the routine unfolded pleasantly and productively and we could see progress toward our goals. On a bad day, it meant living and coping not one day at a time, but one moment at a time. On one of those days when the road stretched too far ahead, I began to wonder, how much is enough? When the need is as all-encompassing and as never-ending as is the constellation of social skills, how would I know where the teaching and nurturing of those skills would cross the line into the repair mode? Where lay the boundary between providing my son the galaxy of services and opportunities he needed and, well, bombardment? Barely five years old, he put in rigorous six-hour days in a developmental kindergarten with afternoon inclusion, speech therapy three days a week, adaptive PE, and one-on-one occupational therapy. Yes, we could go on making the rounds of after-school supplemental therapies, tutorings, and social activities. But I had serious misgivings about what sort of message it sent.

Something is wrong with me.

On the day I first became a mother, our pediatrician told me, "Trust your instincts. You know more than you think you know." Now I chose to follow that advice. I pulled Bryce out of everything but school. I did it because I believed that the pace, the manner, and the context in which we taught him were parts of the skill-building equation as crucial as the skill itself. Force-feeding without creating relevance, without building a framework for him to understand the why behind his social behavior, would bring forth a gag response. The environment in which he would best be able to learn would not be one of incessant pressure and demand. My job was to create that foundation where social awareness could flourish and he could develop genuine self-esteem, like himself, and be comfortable inside his own skin. With those underpinnings, I trusted that he would more easily learn social skills on his unique timetable, not one that I or others had lifted from books or charts or comparisons to other children. I wasn't sure I was doing the right thing, but with Bryce there did seem to be a direct relationship between the pace of teaching, his growing self-awareness, and his self-esteem. His down time was his recharging time. It enabled him to exercise some choice over a portion of his life and consequently, to be willing to give 100% at school. "Bravo," said his paraeducator. "You wouldn't believe how many exhausted kids I see. Like all kids, they need time to just be kids."

Bryce, who by thirteen had succeeded at social interaction in settings ranging from team sports to school dances, was a splendid example of what a child with autism can achieve when healthy self-esteem leads the way. How many, many miles along the spectrum we traveled to get there, sometimes trudging, sometimes tripping the light fantastic. In hindsight I can see that my relentless reinforcing of his self-esteem proved an enormous factor in his willingness to be nudged out of his comfort zone, and to expand that comfort zone. Not yet out of middle school, he had the jaw-dropping—for any kid—ability to deflect teasing and cruelty with the perspective that the insulter "needs to work on his manners" or "has some growing up to do."

Teaching social awareness as an overall concept may feel over-whelming, but as with any large task, you'll be more effective if you separate and clarify your goals, address one goal at a time, start small, and build upon incremental successes. Remove obstacles (usually sensory, language, or self-esteem issues) and throw out preconceived, stereotypical measures of what constitutes progress, the definition of which is sure to be a moving target.

Separating goals and keeping them manageable is of the essence, because where messages overlap, you can't expect your child to be able to sort the primary goal from the secondary one. If you want your child to be a pleasant, involved member of the family at dinner, recognize that several intersecting goals are involved. To isolate the social component, you may need to provide adaptive seating and utensils, eliminate foods (his and others'), smells and sounds that offend his senses, and make concerted efforts to include him in the conversation. Ensure that his time at the dinner table is not an exercise in unpleasant smells and enforced two-bite tastings, lectures about manners and the incomprehensible prattling of the group. If the goal is socialization, separate it from food goals or fine motor processing goals. I've had to walk that talk. At various times in my kids' lives, they ate breakfast in their bedrooms. The commotion of the morning routine rattled them, and the goal at that time of day was nutrition, not socialization. This temporary accommodation, one of many we made along the way, lasted a few months, not forever. And let me tell you where this patient separation of goals got us. The year Bryce was twelve, we celebrated my birthday as a family in one of the most elegant white-tablecloth restaurants in town. The boys loved it, and I will experience few moments more magical than watching Bryce stride confidently up to the piano bar, five-dollar tip in hand to ask the piano man, "Could you please play 'Stardust' for my mom? It's her birthday." The many years of slow-but-steady acclimation melted away.

There's no pill, potion, or recipe for instilling social capability. It builds, phoenix-like, upon itself particle by particle, day by day. "To the top of the mountain, one step at a time," advises the old proverb. We're not Moses, so there won't be tablets at the summit—if there is a summit—but if there were they might look something like this:

1. Eradicate the thought of "fix."

2. Build your child's self-esteem as a foundation for social risk-taking and a shield against the unkindness of others.

3. Focus on social thinking as the means to developing social skills. Learning to consider the thoughts and feelings of people in her environment and working to maintain a balance within social situations will smooth the way for generalization of skills across situations and settings.

4. Create circumstances in which she can practice social skills and succeed, not intermittently, not occasionally, but constantly.

5. Be specific in defining your social skill goals, and beware of goals that overlap or conflict.

6. Start at your child's real level of social processing, not a perceived or assumed one. Some of our kids with advanced vocabularies and elevated IQs fool us into thinking their social abilities are as developed. In most cases, they're not.

7. Keep teaching increments small. Build as you go.

8. Maintain an open-ended definition of what constitutes progress. Two steps forward/one step back is still growth to be celebrated.

9. Provide a reasonable out for social risk-taking situations. You want him to try the church choir or after-school Lego club or volunteering at the pet shelter, but if after several sessions he hates it, praise him for trying, affirm that it's okay to stop, and move on to something else.

10. Remember that social rules and social expectations change over time and within contexts. A socially appropriate behavior for a child of five may be inappropriate for a teenager. What is okay

in the school cafeteria may not be okay in a restaurant or when visiting someone's home.

Fitting into our social world requires a tremendous amount of effort on your child's part. He does the best he can with the abilities and social quotient he has. Despite the nuances he doesn't get, he does know when you believe in him and when that belief falters.

"To the top of the mountain, one step at a time." One of my son Connor's favorite children's books told the story of Sir Edmund Hillary and his Sherpa guide Tenzing Norgay, the first people to reach the summit of Mt. Everest. We talked about the controversy over the years regarding which one of them had put their foot on the top first. Amid speculation that Tenzing arrived at the summit a step or two ahead of the more famous Sir Edmund Hillary, Tenzing's son Jamling told *Forbes* magazine in 2001: "I did ask him, and he said, 'You know, it's not important, Jamling. We climbed as a team.'" Like Tenzing, you've been climbing this mountain for many years. Like Hillary, your child is making his first ascent. Be his Sherpa, knowing and helping him see that the view along the way can be spectacular.

Chapter Nine

Identify what triggers my meltdowns.

Here's something you may not believe but will by the end of this chapter: there can be innumerable reasons why a child with autism melts down, blows up, loses it, goes crackerdog. Being bratty, petulant, obstinate, or spoiled is so far down the list of possibilities that I can't even see it without my binoculars.

We've already faced the unvarnished bottom line: all behavior springs from a reason, and all behavior is communication. A meltdown is a clear message from a child who is not able to tell you in any other way that something in his environment has caused his delicate neurology to go haywire. Even the child whose verbal skills are adequate in an ordinary setting can lose his voice when under stress. For the limited-verbal or nonverbal child, there may be no choice other than behavior, particularly if she's been provided no alternate functional communication system. Regardless of the child's verbal skills, it will be easier for you to keep your wits about you if you remember, always, that it is not within his control. He does not make a conscious choice to melt down. Thinking for even a moment that the child somehow wants the kind of negative attention he gets from a meltdown is illogical and counterproductive.

Square One for us has to be the belief that this child would interact appropriately if he could, but he has neither the social cognition, the sensory integrative abilities, nor the language to achieve it. If this is not your current mindset, it may take conscious practice to get there. With practice, the assumption that there is a trigger, and the curiosity and tenacity to delve for it can become second nature. Many other ideas we've discussed in this book come together here: sensory overload, can't versus won't, inadequate expressive speech, social processing challenges. As you search for triggers, never forget that whatever the underlying cause, your child likely cannot articulate it.

When I say all behavior has a reason, I mean an explanation, an underlying cause. Seeking out reasons can be laborious and challenging. It's not the same as coming up with an excuse for the behavior. An excuse is merely an attempt at justification, and may or may not have any truth behind it. Scrutinize this statement:

"He doesn't want to. He could (behave/sit still/cooperate) if he wanted to."

See how it lets the speaker off the hook, excuses him or her from the harder work of finding an underlying cause? How many, many times we've heard the cliché, "You can do anything if you want to badly enough." Right. That's why we know people who can time-travel, or live to be 300 years old. Can a blind child copy off the whiteboard, if he wants to badly enough? If that sounds familiar, good. Because we're back at Chapter Three, distinguishing between won't and can't. Lack of motivation isn't always the reason for noncompliance. All the motivation in the world may still require patient, sustained instruction and/or assistive technology. We can't (and won't) use "he just doesn't want to" as the rationalization for turning away from more arduous but more effective intervention.

Many will be the wearying moment when the root cause of your child's meltdown won't be immediately evident. There may never be a time in your life when it's more incumbent upon you to become a detective, that is, to ascertain, become aware of, diagnose, discover, expose, ferret out. Baffling behaviors always have a root cause, so you will not be tilting at windmills, Don Quixote-style. It does require that you be detailed, curious, and thorough in your search for that cause. You must be biology detective, psychology sleuth, and environmental investigator.

Meltdown triggers tend to cluster into several areas. If you can pinpoint the trigger, you can prevent the meltdown rather than trying to interrupt or extinguish it once it's in progress (rarely possible). Think of the old Chinese adage: give a man a fish and he eats for a day; teach him how to fish and he eats for a lifetime. Your ability to identify your child's triggers is the first step in helping him identify them himself. Self-regulation can follow.

Let's look at five trigger clusters.

- Sensory overload
- Physical/physiological triggers
  - Food allergies or sensitivities
  - Sleep disturbances

- Gastrointestinal problems
- Inadequate nutrition
- Biochemical imbalances
- Unarticulated illness or injury
- Emotional triggers
- Frustration
  - Disappointment
  - Maltreatment
  - Sense of unfairness
- Poor examples from adults

Sensory overload

As discussed throughout this book, always look for sensory issues first.

The year Bryce was three, we celebrated my birthday at a relative's home, a familiar place to him. Nevertheless, halfway through the evening he began to career through the house in agitation, and when I attempted to calm him, his arms lashed wildly, raking cat-like scratches around my face. Time to go, too soon, but that's the way it was. I gathered up coats and toys. "Wait," said a usually understanding relative. "Are you going to let a three-year-old dictate the evening to the rest of the family?" I knew what he meant. He wanted me to enjoy the evening and the special attention he felt I deserved. But yes, the three-year-old's needs would detour the evening. It didn't negate that we had a lovely time up to that point. And no, he was not dictating. He was communicating. Because his verbal language wasn't there yet, I had to search for meaning in his behavior. The aggression drained out of him as soon as we left. He wasn't being petulant. He was in pain.

The crux of this story is, I knew something was hurting him. It never occurred to me that he would try to ruin my evening. That made no sense. He was in a familiar place with people he knew, loved, and normally enjoyed. Clearly, something was amiss. Too much unfiltered noise? A different, quease-inducing smell? Overtired, too many people? I didn't know and it didn't matter. The most important thing was to end the discomfort before it became the last thing he remembered and the first thing he associated with that venue.

Physical/physiological triggers

- Food allergies and intolerances

These terms are sometimes used interchangeably, but they are not the same thing. An allergy is an abnormally acute immune-system response. An intolerance (sometimes called non-allergic hypersensitivity) is a drug-like reaction to a substance, the degree of response to which varies from person to person (e.g., two red jelly beans may incite hyper or aggressive behavior in one child, whereas another may be able to tolerate a handful). Plenty of evidence exists that both can cause aggressive, belligerent or moody behavior in children. The list of possible offending substances includes anything that goes into the mouth. Common culprits are food dyes, preservatives and other additives, milk, nuts, strawberries, citrus, shellfish, eggs, wheat, corn, and soy.

To detect a substance that may be affecting your child's behavior, keep a food diary of everything he eats for a week, making note of times when behaviors occur. If you see a pattern of problematic behavior after the lunchtime peanut butter sandwich, consider eliminating wheat or nuts from your child's diet for two weeks. Eliminate one substance at a time; phase it out slowly if it's a favorite. Did behaviors diminish after elimination of the food? Test your results by reintroducing a small amount of the food, gradually increasing the dose, seeing if and at what point the behavior returns.

- Sleep disturbances

Behavior problems are sure to follow the child who is chronically exhausted. If you've already tried the usual tactics— setting an inviolable bedtime routine, elimination of naps, "spraying for monsters," avoiding overstimulation—consider our now-familiar nemesis, sensory problems. Could it be:

- Noisy clocks, furnaces, or plumbing? Weather noises such as gurgling gutters, branches scraping against window or roof?
- Scratchy sheets, blankets, or pajamas? Even new items can feel and smell wrong, especially if you've taken away an old favorite.
- Competing smells of laundry products and toiletries?
- Proprioceptive insecurity? She may feel lost in space in her bed. A mummy-style sleeping bag, guardrail, tent or canopy with privacy curtains might help.

- Gastrointestinal problems

For reasons not fully understood, children with autism seem to experience a higher than typical instance of misery-inducing gastrointestinal problems. Your child may be voicing her pain through extreme behavior. Acid reflux (heartburn) can cause esophageal pain, sleep disruption and abdominal discomfort. Constipation and its complications (impaction, encopresis), diarrhea and chronic flatulence have social as well as physiological implications. More serious illnesses such as Crohn's disease, ulcerative colitis, and irritable bowel syndrome (IBS) require ongoing medical supervision. The nonverbal or minimally verbal child's inability to articulate her suffering or cooperate with typical testing are reasons why many children go undiagnosed.

- Inadequate nutrition

Remember the old computer term GIGO— garbage in, garbage out? A child may be eating a lot, but if it's of low nutritive value, his brain may be starving, acutely affecting his behavior. An easy way to improve nutrition is to become conscious of eating foods closer to their original condition. Processed white flour and white sugar products, processed meats, soda, and fruit-flavored drink products are nutrient-low while high in fat, salt, sugar, and chemicals. If behavior deteriorates early in the day, could skipping breakfast be the culprit?

As with allergy identification, make dietary changes s-l-o-w-l-y. A kamikaze-style wipeout of your child's favorite foods is a guaranteed recipe for failure.

- Biochemical imbalances

This can include anything and everything: too much/not enough stomach acid, bile irregularities, vitamin or mineral deficiencies, yeast or bacterial imbalance. It may manifest as anxiety, depression, aggression, weight fluctuations, sleep problems, phobias, and skin problems.

- Unarticulated illness or injury

Ear infections and broken bones are examples of excruciatingly painful conditions that may be impossible for a child with limited verbal ability to adequately communicate.

Emotional triggers

- Frustration

Frustration comes when she's trying but not able to meet your (or her own) expectations and goals. Maybe she does not understand the expectation, or maybe it is too high, unachievable. Maybe it's achievable but she doesn't understand why it's necessary or relevant, or maybe she doesn't have the social, motor, or language skills to accomplish it.

I'll never forget a story I heard years ago about a whirling dervish of a girl with ADHD, nine years old. Her teacher proposed a deal, a reward for meeting a behavioral goal. If the girl could "be good" for three weeks, the teacher would buy her an ice cream cone. The girl reported to her therapist: "Is she kidding? I can't 'be good' for three hours, let alone three weeks. And besides, I don't like ice cream."

The goal: unrealistic, out of reach.

Guidance offered to help in accomplishing the goal: none.

The reward: irrelevant, and nowhere near equal in value to the effort required.

Here's a scenario more constructive times six: Teacher and student (1) meet one-on-one and (2) discuss and agree to (3) a specific, (4) short-range goal (5) that is achievable and (6) has a meaningful motivator as a reward. For instance, the student will work toward remaining in her seat or other designated spot during silent reading time, which is the twenty minutes following lunch recess (short period of time following a physical-release outlet offers best chance of success). She'll start with five-minute increments and work up from there. Success will earn her a token toward computer time, a movie pass, or other mutually-agreed-upon end result that is attractive to her.

For most children, experiencing success results in positive momentum. As her successes build, her frustration will ebb, and so will the upsetting outbursts.

- Disappointment

Disappointment comes when someone he counted upon didn't come through; an event anticipated didn't happen. While a typically-developing child may be able to roll with the punches when schedules or events change, the child with autism depends upon routine and familiarity. Accommodating abrupt changes of direction in his day requires skills he may not yet have and can cause disruption from which it can take hours to recover. Disappointment is a matter of degree for every individual, and it may be a very tough sled to arrive at the point where you understand and empathize with your child's perspective. To you, it's a blip in the routine; to him, a malevolent threat to emotional equilibrium. Disappointments may be unpredictable: the store is out of his favorite juice, the usual route to school is detoured because of road repair, his TV show is preempted for a breaking news report, a play date is cancelled because Addie is sick. Others can be circumvented with forethought and planning. Tell him the pool at this year's vacation hotel will not have a diving board and show him a picture from the hotel brochure or website. Have Grandma tell him she will be serving apple pie instead of pumpkin at Thanksgiving this year. Explain that Calvin the beloved Camp Counselor won't be back this year but go to meet Nathan the New Guy before the session starts.

- Maltreatment

She's being attacked, provoked, or teased by peers, siblings, or other adults. Whether in your home, your school, or any other setting, there is only one acceptable position: zero tolerance. How user-friendly is your child's environment in this regard? Your child with autism has neither the verbal sophistication nor the social acuity to adequately defend herself. Angry meltdowns are only the beginning. Close on their heels may be anxiety, depression, and chronic fatigue. Taking action to protect your child or student in such situations is mandatory.

Our elementary school's administration and teaching staff ferociously enforced a policy declaring the school a No Put-Down Zone, dealing with incidences of unkindness in any degree promptly and decisively. We never took our school's policy for granted, not for a minute. At another school, a mother told me a different story:

> My son started first-grade with positive, consistent feedback from us, but quickly deteriorated under daily physical abuse from his peers. Both the teacher and the

principal reacted to my repeated concerns by admonishing me to stop being overprotective. My son needed to learn how to take care of himself; these things happen between kids and you can't always be there to save them. He needed to learn to stand up for himself, stop being such a baby, focus more, work harder, listen better, do as told, try harder, be more responsive, and on, and on, and on.

I crumble inside every time I hear a shameful account such as this one. "These things happen between kids"? Of course they do, when the adults in charge continue to allow it. Whether the perpetrators are classmates, siblings, or other adults, our declining to take action declares our choice to allow harassment to flourish. And if the victim responds with anger or aggression—duh!

So here's the chant again: just because he can't tell you it's happening doesn't mean that it isn't. Most harassment happens out of the hearing range of parents, teachers, and other adults: on the bus, in the bathroom, in the halls, on the playground. Teach your child or student, as soon as he is able, to 1) protest appropriately, "Stop! I don't like that," and 2) tell a trusted adult.

- Sense of unfairness

"Fair" is one of those hazy, imprecise terms perplexing to our kids with autism. He doesn't think in terms of fair or unfair, but does know he's having trouble balancing his needs with the rules. Adults often think that *fair* means impartial, equitable, unbiased. Family rules, school rules, and team rules apply to each sibling, student, or teammate equally. But autism un-levels the playing field. It potholes the field. All things are not being equal. So our thinking on the subject of *fair* must change. Here it is:

Fair does not mean everything is equal.

Fair is when everyone gets what they need.

Poor examples from adults

I once worked for a general manager who would occasionally invoke an indelicate metaphor when he wanted to place responsibility in someone else's lap. He didn't care for the usual sports idioms like "the ball is in their court." Rather, he liked to "put the turd back in their pocket." It always turned a few ears pink. Vivid, unpleasant imagery, but sometimes that's what it takes to focus attention on something from which we'd rather turn away.

The mirror can be unforgiving, but any examination of our child's undesirable behavior has to start with a look at our own. "Speak when you are angry and you will make the best speech you'll ever regret," said Laurence J. Peter, author of *The Peter Principle: Why Things Always Go Wrong.* If you react with anger and frustration to your child or student's meltdowns, you're modeling the very behavior you want him or her to change. It's incumbent upon you as an adult, at all times and in every situation, to refrain from responding in kind. Be your own behavior detective. Figure out what triggers your own boiling point and interrupt the episode before you reach that point. When your thermostat zooms skyward, better to temporarily remove yourself from the situation. Tell your child, "You're angry [frustrated, upset] and I am, too. I need to be away from you [or, by myself] for a few minutes so that I can calm down. I am going to my room [or outside or upstairs] for now, but I will come back to you and we can talk about it."

Be aware of the many ways in which we unwittingly make a bad situation worse. Derision—laughing at someone's pain or misfortune, projecting a serves-you-right attitude. Sometimes we make unfair, irrelevant comparisons, such as "Your sister never did this." We launch into kitchen-sink arguments, bringing up bygone incidents: "This is just like the time you ____." We may make unproven accusations: "You must have done this. Nobody else would have." As with any difficult situation, planning is key. At a time when you are calm, think through how you can better handle the next incident. Then write down your plan, keep it in an accessible place, and refer to it periodically to keep it fresh in your mind.

"How much more grievous are the consequences of anger than the causes of it," said first-century Roman educator Marcus Aurelius. From time to time, a parent will tell me, with strident conviction, that hitting their child was the only way to get through to him or her, and that it worked because the child "turned out okay." I can't begin to understand what "turned out okay" means when the child in question has yet to reach adulthood, or even adolescence. Such parents usually try to put lipstick on this pig by calling it spanking, swatting, paddling, or corporal punishment, but by any name, it's an aggressive act perpetrated almost invariably in anger. Sometimes it happens in a momentary loss of self-control, sometimes with the mistaken conviction that it will somehow, without the actual effort of instruction, teach appropriate behavior.

My guess is that most readers who have come this far into this book aren't so inclined anyway, but have encountered people who are. I've got your back here; consider what follows to be your ammo against that vocal family member, neighbor, or bystander who feels the pressing need to let you know that all your kid needs is a good smack.

Consider:

- Does spanking follow careful weighing of alternative responses and a reasoned decision that, yes, striking someone one-quarter our size is logical, provides a good example for them to follow, and will produce the desired long-term result? Can we be sure that it teaches the child what she did wrong? Does it give her the knowledge and skills to correct the behavior? Or does spanking spring from aggravation, wrath, and desperation? Does it foster respect and understanding, or humiliation and bewilderment? Does it enhance the child's ability to trust us?

- Is it a behavior we want the child to emulate? The same behavior perpetrated toward a coworker or neighbor would be called assault and battery, earning us a free ride in a squad car. Under the Geneva conventions, we are not allowed to apply corporal punishment to prisoners of war. Why should it be okay to do it to a child?

We cannot rail against bullying at school or on the Internet while allowing it within the home or family. We've just discussed the importance of teaching a child to report maltreatment to a trusted adult. Trust is not an entitlement a child owes the authority figures in his life. It must be earned, and once earned, maintained on a daily basis. Whatever actions you must take or refrain from, you want to be one of those trusted adults in a child's life, because if you're not, the horrifying long-term consequence is that he may not tell you if, in the future, another adult behaves aggressively or abusively toward him.

Anger is contagious, and in the end, it costs us: in time lost, energy expended, trust violated, self-worth stunted, feelings wounded, and long-term results unattained. Yet, anger is also inevitable in the human experience. Learning to handle anger with proactive self-control and dignity ultimately empowers both you and, through your example, your child.

Ferreting out the causes and consequences of troubling behaviors has a formal name. A Functional Behavior Analysis (FBA) assesses specific behaviors based on their ABCs: the antecedent (cause or trigger), the behavior itself, and the consequence (what happens to the child as a result of the behavior). An FBA can be a formal process carried out in the school setting by trained personnel or an informal one, i.e., parental home observation. Websites such as www.wrightslaw.com and others can guide you through the process. The idea behind an FBA is that, once identified, the antecedents and consequences of a behavior can be altered or modified by teaching the child more appropriate behavior. That's such an important piece of the equation that I am going to repeat it: behavior modification doesn't stop at interrupting or extinguishing an undesirable behavior.

However baffling or distasteful to you, a child's behavior happens for a reason and fills a need. Squelching a behavior without addressing the underlying cause will only result in another behavior rising to fill the need.

Learning to deal with your child's meltdowns isn't easy. But it's one piece of the autism puzzle where answers await those who are up for the hunt. I found the process wondrous. The better I got at identifying and respecting Bryce's triggers, the more peaceful life became. The frightening several-times-a-day meltdowns diminished to several times a week, morphed briefly into occasional passive-aggressive responses, then vanished completely. Completely. It's been many years since I've thought about it in any manner other than being grateful for how we faced down something so ugly and overcame it. My recall of those bad old days is fading. It's one of the most impressive special effects I've ever seen.

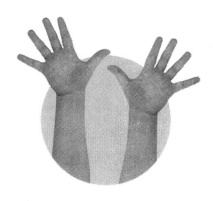

Chapter Ten

Love me unconditionally.

"The difference between heaven and earth is not so much altitude but attitude."

These words, from the book *The Power of Unconditional Love* by Ken Keys, Jr., form the overarching sentiment for everything I believe about raising a child with autism, and they come from a man who lived that difference every day. Polio put Keys in a wheelchair the last fifty years of his life, so he knew a little about living with a so-called disability. It didn't stop him from writing fifteen books about loving life, finding happiness in what you already have, and keeping your focus forward. Unconditional love, he contends, is based on dualities, the most encompassing of which is that in order to love someone else, we have to love ourselves, "accepting all parts of ourselves." What better example to set for your child?

Unconditional love is both magical and attainable. No question, the challenges of raising atypical children can seem staggering. Face in the dirt, knife in the heart, down for the count. Rising above and firmly pushing aside our own fears, disappointments, expectations, and lost dreams can seem like a mission of overwhelming enormity. Your child's limitations become yours—the places you can't take him, the social settings he can't handle, the people he can't relate to, the food he won't eat. Yeah, it can be a long list. But it has been and continues to be a cherished privilege to claim our two boys as mine and to love them unconditionally. It's taught me profound lessons about how excruciating it can be to keep that kind of love in the crosshairs at all times.

It takes courage to admit that you're scared, feel cheated, heartsick, depleted. Wanting out of that matrix and not knowing how to start. Here's how: by knowing you can do this. It's already in you.

In the early days of contemplating what Bryce's life and my family's would be like with autism in our midst, I could not deny the fact that it could be much worse. All around me were people who had confronted just that. Close friends had lost their precious two-year-old daughter to a heart defect, a life-shattering event far more devastating than anything autism threw at our family. It underscored the pricelessness of what we had—hope. To travel hopefully, Robert Louis Stevenson wrote in 1881, is a better thing than to arrive.

Bryce taught me that happiness does not come from getting what you want, but from wanting what you already have. It is the greatest gift I have ever been given. A friend once asked me, how do you get there? What do you think is the secret of your success?

It's no secret. It's just this: accept your situation without bitterness. Play the cards you drew with grace and optimism. Bitterness can be a formidable foe; overcoming it can be a daily exercise. Some of us make it, some of us don't.

Back in Chapter Three, I spoke of a parent who claimed that because of autism, he could not have a relationship with his son. He knew his son would end up in prison. I talked and reasoned and pleaded away the afternoon with this man, begging him to see that he was setting up a self-fulfilling prophecy. Couldn't he take one baby step out, imagining a different outcome for his belligerent but bright child—ten minutes of floor time, coming to school once a month, finding a restaurant they both liked? I think he loved his son but to the child it no doubt felt conditional, dependent upon a certain kind of behavior, even if there were organic reasons why he could not comply. In the end, they both lost out. This dad could not move beyond his bitterness and grief.

Grief is real. Getting stuck in that grief—that is the true tragedy, not that your child has autism.

Try to imagine yourself in the world of your own child or student, with its incessant sensory invasion, eddies of incomprehensible language swirling around him, the impatience and disregard of "normal" people. You face the same question I did so many long years ago. If I did not swallow my own anguish and be the one to step up for him, who would?

Do you dare imagine your child's life as an adult after you're gone? That's a harsh question, and it's the one that keeps me on track every day of my life. What kind of life awaits an adult who has limited language ability, doesn't comprehend the law and law enforcement, the banking system, public transportation, workplace issues such as punctuality, basic etiquette, respectful communication, group dynamics? To what level of quality can life rise without at least a few meaningful interpersonal relationships, meaningful work, meaningful pastimes or hobbies? Most children grow up assuming that these things will be the components of their adult lives. For the child with autism, such a future can exist, but not without the collaborative intervention of adults committed 100% to the idea that being everything one can be is the birthright of every child.

For some cosmic, not-to-be-understood reason, I was blessed with the serenity to bypass the denial and the anger and the self-pity that frequently come unbidden and unwelcome when we learn our child has a so-called disability. That is not to say that I don't endure my own bouts with melancholy, that I don't fall prey to what I call the Knife-to-the-Heart moments. These are the times when the rest of the world seems intent on letting you know that your child is different and apart. Often there's no conscious malice; it happens because the mainstream population is streaming about their business in mainstream fashion, which doesn't or can't include your child. Other times, the spite is intentional—the offhand child-cruel remark, the birthday party that everyone else is invited to, the snubs on the bus. Then come the questions he asks you as he begins to figure out that he is different. I thought that if I endured enough Knife-to-the-Heart moments, I would develop scar tissue or the ability to laugh them off. I haven't. But as both my boys moved with increasing grace toward maturity and independence, those moments became fewer, farther between and more fleeting. The power they hold over me weakened over time.

Loving Bryce unconditionally required, at different times, making peace with what seemed like reduced opportunities. As a young child, he didn't seem to want conventional friendships, play dates and sleepovers, wasn't interested in the usual after-school activities like soccer or choir. He couldn't tolerate large-scale shows or sporting events in arenas or stadiums. Travel had to be carefully orchestrated. Curiously, I can't say I missed these things because he was a happy child who felt good about himself. Still I pondered. And still I asked a lot of questions.

My children's middle school years arrived, and there I sat one morning in our psychologist's office, bewildered yet again at my son's social development, which seemed to meander all over the landscape without ever treading the established path. During this meeting, after the practical and the actionable suggestions, the psychologist gave me this memorable advice: "And remember: all children, all people, unfold in their own time. This may not be his time. His time will come."

We gave (and still give) Bryce the time and space to do that. Those times did come. As he grew older, he swam on a recreational league swim team and ran on the school track team, acted in community theater, surfed and backpacked, zoomed around on his bike, enjoyed Cub Scout activities, read Harry Potter. And he did all these things right on time—his time. It may have been a couple of years behind the typical timeline, but he did them as successfully as any kid, and what's more, the minute he did, we magically forgot that he ever hadn't.

Every day of Bryce's childhood, I told him that he was an interesting and wonderful person and that I was the luckiest mommy who ever lived. In the beginning, I believed it enough to start saying it, but as time went on a marvelous thing happened. It became fact to me. I began to actively look for things about him to articulate. I told him I was proud of how readily he shared treats and privileges with others, how I admired his devotion to his school work, how I enjoyed the clever associations he made as he pulled minute details out of movies and related them to his real life. How I could trust him because he never lied, how nicely he took care of himself with healthy food choices and good hygiene. In time, it became part and parcel of his self-image. And because he believed it, he grew into a young man with remarkable aplomb, self-confidence, empathy and work ethic, and who likes himself —not necessarily the typical hallmarks of autism.

Think of it as affirmative brainwashing. The more you articulate your child's strengths and gifts, the more both of you grow to believe it.

If you can get to a place where you believe, accept, and put true unconditional love into practice, you will find yourself infused with a commanding energy on behalf of your child. Without it, you're going to be running this race with a nasty pebble in your shoe. It may be a hundred-dollar shoe, but that pebble will ensure that your focus dwells on the ever-more-painful wound to your extremity, rather than on the span of the road ahead or the beauty of your surroundings. It's a simple choice: let the irritant remain until it cripples you, or remove it and head for the horizon. With the full force of your commitment behind the rudder, your child's time will come.

The fast track, record pace, maximum velocity, instant gratification culture of the twenty-first century is not the hand your child drew. He or she beckons you down that road less traveled, the road the poet Frost tells us is "just as fair, and having perhaps the better claim." It is perhaps the better claim because, at the end of this book, we have come full circle, back to where we started: neither you nor he yet know what the scope of his achievement can be. We can't see the end of the road, not only because it's full of dips, downgrades, and tricky curves, but because there is no end. An energizing, uplifting thought, or a draining, wearying one—your choice. Henry Ford, that icon of American industrialism, succeeded in spectacular fashion because he sought out people "who have an infinite capacity to not know what can't be done."

I want to leave you with the wise words of Joshua Liebman's "A Parent's Commandments." Our family committed to these directives at the naming ceremonies we held for both of our sons shortly after their births, joyful occasions during which everything seemed possible for them. We could never have imagined how prescient these words would be:

> Give your child unconditional love, a love that is not
> dependent on report cards, clean hands or popularity.
>
> Give your child a sense of your whole-hearted acceptance,
> acceptance of his human frailties as well as
> his abilities and virtues.
>
> Give him a sense of truth; make him aware of himself
> as a citizen of the universe in which there are many
> obstacles as well as fulfillments.
>
> Give your child permission to grow up and make his
> own life independent of you.
>
> These are the laws of honoring your child.

Please join me in doing this for your child. Along your road less traveled, it will make all the difference.

Afterword

One of Bryce's paraeducators, a professional of many years' experience, looked back on her years with Bryce and told me, "All that time I thought I was teaching him but now I see it was he who was teaching me." I feel the same way. *Ten Things* only scratches the surface of what I have learned from Bryce. But I always return like a boomerang to a certain core of thought.

"Whether you think you can or whether you think you can't, you're probably right." That's Henry Ford again, a person who some think occupied a spot on the autism/Asperger's/ADHD spectrum. An authentic diagnosis is lost to history, but the diagnosis is less important than the message: what you choose to believe about your child's autism might be the single biggest factor in his outcome.

If that sounds like a challenge, it is. Run with it; the wind is at your back. It will keep you moving forward and that's where the action and answers are. Why your child has autism may be a question without an answer. What you can do about it, how you can make a difference, and where to seek the resources to guide you are questions with concrete answers that will keep you going for the rest of your life.

It doesn't matter how you get to the point of being a Believer. I sometimes can't believe how I got there. It reads like an allegory, my own personal parable, and it goes like this:

I'm going back to school. I'll be studying at my beloved alma mater and it's exhilarating to be back. Though more than twenty years have passed, much of what I originally loved about it remains unchanged. It's still a little strip of a town. It still has its quaint square for a downtown.

But there's a kink in my homecoming. And it's literally about home. Though I started looking months in advance, I can't nail down an apartment. One is supposed to be available but when I come with my stuff, someone is already living there. Another turns out to be on the far side of nowhere and it's cramped, dilapidated, and stinky. One landlord wants me to wait two weeks; there might be an availability. The term gets underway and I have nowhere to go but the back seat of my car. I'm too old for dormitory life but I've run out of options. The dorms are fully booked, I'm told, but I can stay in this one room until the student with the reservation shows up.

Thus begins a harrowing game of human checkers as I must move from room to room every few days, clearing out for the next legitimate name on the waiting list, moving to a space temporarily vacated by the latest dropout. When I get shoved one last time to the end unit of this tenuous tenement, will I simply tumble out the hall window and vanish into the Vinca major?

And I have another problem, just as pressing. With the constant distraction of my homelessness, half the term has slipped away. I've skipped some classes—a lot of classes. In shock, I realize that it's too late to recover by the end of the term. By missing so much class, I don't have the background to complete the coursework and I have no relationships with the professors upon which to fall back and create alternative solutions. I am going to fail, resoundingly, for the first time in my academic career. It is humiliation on a level I could never have imagined.

And then I wake up.

More curious than disturbing, the dream kept popping up every few months. Its message seemed consistent. I read books on dream interpretation, but found nothing to explain the lack-of-housing component.

An easy-going acquaintance of mine, who seemed down to earth in every way, urged me to go see a professional psychic she knew. Laurie could figure it out in a snap, she said, and wouldn't it be nice to know? What if it was something important?

Laurie, a former critical care nurse, ran a thriving psychic consultancy in an upscale suburb. She had a large number of business clients on retainers and she conducted extensive workshops. My curiosity won out and I made an appointment for a reading.

She began the session by telling me, "Don't say anything yet. I will tell you what I'm getting from you, and then there will be plenty of time to ask questions." For the first five minutes, she told me things she couldn't possibly know. I was mighty impressed. Now we could get to the question about my dream. She brushed it off in a matter of seconds. "That one's easy," she said. "You're looking for greater intellectual stimulation but can't figure out how to fit it into your life. I see a book published within the next five years."

Yes, and I'll become an Olympic decathlete, too, I thought. It's not what I expected. I pressed on. "I want to ask you about my child," I started hesitantly. "There seems to be something ... extra ... about him." She examined his photo and asked for his birth date. "It's kind of scary," I managed to get out. "Is he an angel or a fairy or something?"

"Oh no," she said. "Not an angel. An angel is a new soul. He is a very old soul."

She talked about past life regression, and I listened impassively. Did I believe this stuff? No, I can't say that I did. But neither did I not believe it. Nobody had ever proven anything to me one way or the other. I'd paid money to hear answers, so it behooved me to listen with an open mind.

"Bryce is a great spiritual leader," she said. "You and he have been together many times in many lifetimes, in different roles: teacher and student, husband and wife, leader and confidante. He trusts you. This time, you're here together as mother and son. This is the role he chose for you. This time."

"He chose me?"

"Yes."

Laurie gave me a tape of our session, telling me to go home and let everything percolate and sift and settle for a few weeks, then listen to our conversation again.

That's what I did. It was hard not to be mesmerized by the idea that he chose me. One night, an entirely ordinary bedtime, we ended the day in the usual way, on his bed with a book. It had been a busy summer day filled with camp and popsicles and grass stains. He was a clear and pleasant tired; it wouldn't be an hour of stories and goodnights. Heavy eyelids descended over his famous blue eyes. In the purplish-gray light, the curve of his cheek and nose and the plane of his skin seemed beyond real. What I was about to do was unfair and unfitting, but I couldn't resist, couldn't fight it. I had to ask him.

"Bryce?"

"Yes?" An all-but-asleep whisper.

"Did you choose me?"

By his silence, I thought he had drifted off. Then, though his eyes did not open, I heard quite clearly:

"Yes, Mom."

Have you ever in your life been confronted with something that caused you to evacuate your senses? The moment would stand forever apart for me because I did not know what to think.

He might have just been tired and wanting me to leave. But I heard something else. I heard it through the haze of my own long-standing skepticism.

What I heard was that more choice was at stake than whether or not I could find verifiable truth in the scenario of him choosing me as a mother. The larger significance lies in what we choose to believe where no tangible evidence exists, and how we will allow that choosing to direct our actions.

When beloved American composer George Gershwin passed away, the novelist John O'Hara said, "George died on July 11, 1937, but I don't have to believe that if I don't want to."

We choose to believe that which provides us with what we need to make it through the tough situations. Allowing myself to believe that Bryce had chosen me as his mother, that somehow across time, he believed that I was the one for the job, renewed my determination to do right by him. This thought, if true, confirmed that our belief in each other was eternally circular.

"Whether you think you can or whether you think you can't, you're probably right."

A spectrum's worth of personal difference and one hundred years' time separate Laurie's remarks from Henry Ford's. So disparate are they that the only way they could both have ended up in my lap together is that they are bound by a common truth: that it is choice, not chance, that guides our hand on the helm.

I believe that.

Triumph and Transition

On the evening my husband and I attended our last-ever back-to-school parent night, Bryce had embarked on his final year of high school and we were a light year away from his initial identification as a child with autism. That long-ago year, he attended a supported integrated preschool class. Each Thursday he greeted the teacher with, "One more day, baby," a line from the movie *Little Giants*. On the morning before his first day as a high school senior, Bryce turned to me and said, "One more year, baby."

Seven years after we left that preschool, I wrote an article called *Ten Things Every Child with Autism Wishes You Knew*, which grew into this book. Its ten things spoke for the younger child Bryce had been at the time. Another seven years later, he was eighteen years old and well able to speak for himself so, on the eve of his last year in high school, my role changed. Now I would speak to him, not for him. Thus, another ten things, putting in writing a canon I'd tried to instill in him through the course of his growing years, and that I hoped he would now choose to take with him into adulthood.

You'll notice right away that these ten things aren't autism-specific. That's because the older Bryce grew, the more his autism became only a part of him, a thinking and learning style, not a gargoyle crouched over him dictating his existence, not a defining or even controlling characteristic. He would be the first to tell you that his autism has and always will impose challenges on his life. But he has also cultivated in himself grace and fortitude. He will live these ten things long after his senior year becomes a distant memory.

Ten Things I Want My High School Senior with Autism to Know

Be a role model. Be the kind of senior you appreciated as a freshman, the kind of welcoming, mentoring upperclassman who helped you get off to such a good start. All young people need role models. You had them, now it's your turn to be one. This duty won't end when you graduate. As you prepare to assume the responsibilities and liberties of adulthood, understand that healthy, vibrant communities hinge on citizens who set the example for the generation that follows.

Never compromise your integrity. A lifetime of building a reputation for honesty, trustworthiness, and kindness can be destroyed in an instant. One lie, one act of disloyalty, one infidelity, one thoughtless remark. One "just this once" cheating or pilfering. That's all it takes to damage or ruin relationships of all kinds—family, friends, bosses, coworkers. Trust destroyed takes years to rebuild because *you can't prove a negative* like "I'll never do it again" by anything other than the passage of time.

Don't wish away the moment for the future. You're excited at the thought of exploring college, work, and the world beyond high school. But many wonderful opportunities and experiences await you as part of your senior year. Embrace and savor them. The many small, daily joys of life may pass you by if you are always marking time, waiting for some future event.

Manners count. As our society grows ever more unmannerly, manners may be the very thing that places you a cut above others when vying for a job, a favor, a friendship. Remember your favorite scene in *Ghostbusters* when Bill Murray won't show William Atherton the storage facility "because you did not use the magic word." The Atherton character has to be told that the magic word is "please." Please! Manners are never inappropriate or out of style. Know that many a budding romance has been killed by lax table manners. Curb your use of casual profanity before it becomes so ingrained that it slips out at exactly the wrong moment. ("Nice to meet you, Mr. Smith. Your daughter is f**king awesome!") Because...

There's someone out there for you. Stood up, blown off, misled—it's been hard to watch while mean girls baffle and betray you. But you've cast your eye upon and struck friendships with some lovely young women. Trust your character judgment; it's sound, even though you won't always be right. No one is. We don't know when or where your special someone will show up, but the wait will be worth it. Enjoy and learn from your experiences with the medley of relationships you have with many women—friends, campus acquaintances, co-workers. Younger, older, common interests, different interests and backgrounds. And know also that your value, your measure of success in life, does not depend upon becoming half of a pair.

Know when to ask for help. Your drive to become an independent adult is strong, but be aware of the critical difference between being strong and being headstrong. Asking for help and learning from those who help you is a mark of strength and maturity, not weakness or inability. Ask, ask, ask—that's where you'll find the knowledge and opportunities that will bring you the independence you so desire. What you gain by asking is what will elevate you to the next level—being able to help others when they come to you and ask.

Have a dream, but also be realistic—and employable. You want to be a screenwriter. I had the writing jones myself, so I get it. No one should ever be without dreams and goals, but you will need marketable job skills to support yourself while you pursue the dream. Even your own mom had a "day job"—for twenty-five years—before becoming a full-time writer.

Keep perspective. Your autism has placed challenges upon you, and it will continue to. That's why it's important to remain ever aware of the vast range of human conditions around you. I cannot say it better than the words of "Desiderata": "If you compare yourself with others, you may become vain or bitter, for always there will be greater and lesser persons than yourself."

Vote. You've grown up listening to me hiss at people, "If you don't vote, don't complain." Voting is both a privilege and an obligation. The issues are complicated and candidates will be manipulative. Don't use the complexity as an excuse not to participate in the process, to do the tough work of learning to distinguish between opinion and fact, to make reasoned decisions about people, and to be a voice on the issues that affect your community.

Finish strong. Remember all your years of running track, where races were decided by who was able to power across the finish line. If you feel a creeping urge to coast toward the end of this year ("senioritis")—don't. Get in the habit of finishing strong. Few traits impress employers more than knowing they can rely on an employee to carry projects through to completion on time and with his full best efforts.

Bryce, you and I have been talking to each other (not always with words) for eighteen years. We've talked about a million things that make up one word—life. The sum of those conversations is there for everyone to see; they are part of the extraordinary man you have become.

From your earliest years, your exceptional work ethic and drive for independence, your innate sense of right and wrong, and your kind and valorous heart became legendary among every teacher, coach, and counselor who ever worked with you. How could I let myself be less than your example? Because of you, I learned to see the world from wondrous vistas I never knew existed. To paraphrase one of our favorite Jack Nicholson lines, "You made me want to be a better mom."

As you cross the threshold of adulthood, you are as solid a person as anyone I have ever known. You are a brave heart, a gentleman, an artist, a scholar, a good citizen, a lover. You are Atticus Finch, Rocky Balboa, Benny Rodriguez and Obi-wan Kenobi all rolled into one.

The world needs you.

Evolution

Shortly after graduating from high school, Bryce adopted a new mantra. "Everyone evolves" became his frequent commentary on the changes transpiring in his own life and the lives of those in the concentric circles rippling around and away from him. When your child is young and his challenges many, imagining him as an adult is a far stretch. But it comes all too soon. The simple messages of childhood collide with the oil-and-water social-emotional brew of adolescence. And the older your child grows, the more she must navigate on her own, and the more her ability to self-advocate becomes critical. Her success as an adult will depend upon her being able to describe the aspects of her autism that impact her ability to learn, communicate, and socialize, and to be able to ask for the kind of help she needs.

149

Barring unthinkable catastrophe, your child with autism *will* become an adult. In the eyes of the law (speaking of American law), it happens the moment the clock strikes midnight on the morning of his eighteenth birthday. Many services will fall away, many legal rights (and liabilities) will be his. Without your knowledge, permission, or approval, your son or daughter will be able to vote, marry, sign a contract, join the military. He or she will be subject to adult laws and law enforcement, will be able to buy tobacco and pornography, consent to or decline medical treatment. You will no longer be able to even discuss his health with his doctor without his written permission. This is not to say that you won't continue to play a significant role in your child's life, advising, guiding, and supporting him. But your *power* to control the events of his life will diminish profoundly.

Transition: it's yours as much as his. How can I describe to you that inevitable moment when your child arrives at legal adulthood, a vortex of pride and apprehension and anticipation and nostalgia? I can only say that it may come as bittersweet to you, depending on where you are on this road to adulthood, whether you've prepared not only your child, but yourself for this "mother of all transitions." Like every transition through which your child passes, it will tow you along in its wake whether you're game for the ride or not. But the proportion of joy to alarm is yours to control.

Preparing your child for productive, self-sufficient adulthood in the grownup version of "least restrictive environment" begins the day your child is born. Because the quality of his tomorrow depends on each today that comes before it, the question of the day, every day, is *how* will your child turn eighteen—as prepared as possible (or at least on the way), or naïve, unskilled, and ill-equipped?

You're familiar now with some of the ups and downs of my family's journey. Let me tell you, as a mom on the other side of the Great Divide between youth and majority, what the run-up to that passage looked like, from one of our lowest moments to a high point from which I hope I never recover.

In the very first hour of our discussion following the formal educational identification of Bryce's autism, his preschool teachers placed the goal of independent adulthood squarely in our sights by labeling him a PIA, Potentially Independent Adult. Finally—a label I could buy into. And more good news: these energetic, progressive teachers and their region-wide class were based in our neighborhood school. We would be able to observe first-hand how the school functioned and whether it would be a good fit for Bryce when he started kindergarten the next year.

Forewarned is forearmed. My search for a better school activated the minute I heard that a primary grade teacher had sneered at one of my son's paraeducators, "And what exactly is it that you expect to accomplish with these kids?" Her question raised plenty of my own and prompted me to look around the rest of the school. I saw a war-weary principal close, but not close enough, to retirement. I saw a teaching staff with low morale, first grades overflowing with upwards of thirty kids, endemic behavior problems unchecked. I knew there had to be a healthier learning and social environment for my son.

I investigated every public and private school within a twenty-five mile radius of our home. We found an outstanding public school that welcomed different learners, and that fed into a better than average middle school. We moved into the district. There Bryce thrived and progressed until seventh grade.

The first inkling of a shift in the collective attitude of some of our IEP team came from a resource teacher who volunteered her opinion on Bryce's employment prospects as an adult, saying that she could "see our friend Bryce doing well in a cubicle doing clearly delineated tasks exactly as he is told." The tone of her voice indicated that she thought she was delivering good news. But Bryce wanted to pursue filmmaking, an outside-the-cubicle profession if ever there was one. Our creeping unease detonated with that year's triennial psychological testing required to maintain his eligibility for special services. Bryce came home one day reporting that a woman he'd never met took him to a room he'd never seen and put a battery of tests in front of him. He didn't know who she was or for what purposes the tests were being given. He was concerned about missing class and raced through the tests, most of which seemed abstract and irrelevant.

The test administrator, a school psychologist, reported back to us that among other things, Bryce's IQ measured out at sixty-nine, a number that carried the designation "borderline."

"Borderline what?" I asked.

"Borderline, you know," she said, "the word that starts with R that we try not to use anymore."

She also pronounced that the services mandated in his IEP were "too much," and that she'd be recommending less. The classroom teachers who worked with Bryce day in and day out hooted in derision and disgust, calling the test results "patently ridiculous" and "wildly inaccurate."

My first call went to the school district head of special education, demanding that he remove the psychologist from our IEP team. (He did, without hesitation.) Then I fought the psychologist's "findings" all the way up the food chain to the district head of the psychology department, who eventually conceded, in writing, that the IQ score of sixty-nine more reflected Bryce's processing *speed* than his intelligence. When I asked, "What does processing speed have to do with intelligence?", he replied, "Nothing." It seemed clear to me that the people in our school system who held our son's future in their hands no longer believed in his quest for independent adulthood.

About this time, a friend asked me if I had heard of Thomas Edison High School and their summer program for middle-schoolers. On the Edison website, I found the description of a high school devoted exclusively to students with learning differences, a program tailor-made for Bryce, right here in our hometown of Portland, Oregon. The summer middle school session would be an ideal introduction. Summer school is no teen's idea of a fun vacation, and Bryce arrived at Edison the first week of July with abject, hangdog reluctance. There he landed in the classroom of Kassie Robinson, a teacher who would change his life in many ways. When we met her on parent night, the first words out of her mouth were, "Well, he's brilliant, but I'm sure you already know that." And Bryce told us, "I need to go to this school. These teachers understand me."

So we came to Thomas Edison High School, where the teaching credo matched my own: "Whatever it takes." On our first parent night, we sat in the art classroom, where the teacher introduced herself with, "All my students succeed. ALL my students succeed." And I turned to my husband Mark and said, "Toto, we're not in Kansas anymore."

At Edison, Bryce joined a community of teens with a rainbow of learning differences (dyslexia, ADD, ADHD, Asperger's, Tourette's, visual perception, and nonverbal learning differences) who shared a common challenge, where stigma and ostracism were all but non-existent and where every student's potential for success was assumed. In this atmosphere of empowerment, Bryce learned to understand precisely how his autism affects his ability to learn and socialize, how to advocate for his learning needs and emotional needs, and how to prioritize, manage his time, and otherwise adapt to the speed bumps his autism presented. He identified as his primary obstacles his slow processing speed and his difficulty retaining auditory information. Recognizing this, he learned, after a lifetime of struggling with math, that he could succeed in the self-paced class the school offered; he earned four years of straight As, never missing an assignment. He learned he could excel at subjects completely new to him, earning the top academic award for American Sign Language during his junior year. He learned he could find personal relevance in vast, intimidating subjects like history; his research paper on the history of action films earned him another top academic award.

His teachers called him a star.

At times his devotion to his work bordered on compulsive, spending long evenings and whole weekends working to the exclusion of all else. His principal intervened, urging him to create some balance in his life. "It takes me longer," Bryce would say simply, adding that no one would ever be allowed the chance to call him a slacker.

He stretched himself socially in ways that he could tolerate. He attended every school dance and joined a 300-member track team where he didn't know a soul. "I like to run," he shrugged. He made one fast friend, a number of acquaintances, and stuck with it for three years. Ms. Robinson directed him into a filmmaking program for youth where he spent every summer of his high school years. During his last summer there, he worked as an intern, coaching new young filmmakers entering the program.

On a lovely spring afternoon toward the end of our four years at Edison, I picked up Bryce after school to take him to get his tuxedo for the prom. During the day, I'd played a few rounds of phone tag with the school's assistant director. As we drove off, Bryce asked, "Did you get a message from Mr. P today?"

Something in his voice made me ask, "Bryce, do I need to pull over?"

And he said, "Yes."

I did.

"Mom," he said, "I'm valedictorian."

Bryce did not arrive at any of these academic, social, or emotional pinnacles in a typical way. He is no genius, nor was he the best-spoken, most outgoing, adventurous, or activist student in his class. Rather, he built his achievements through plain old hard work, hour after painstaking hour, months upon years. His is the triumph of a man who understands and embraces responsibility, and places his highest premium on perseverance and integrity.

At graduation, the assistant director offered this tribute to Bryce:

"More than anything, I want to tell you that this student is humble and classy. When I approached this young man about his accomplishment, he said with enthusiasm and sincerity, 'I want you to know that other students worked hard too. Even though I am being recognized for this award, all of us have worked extremely hard to be able to graduate.' This speaks to his heart, which could easily fill this auditorium."

Bryce responded in his grad speech by thanking his teachers "for teaching me all the things that used to be hard for me, but aren't anymore. To me," he said, "graduating doesn't mean you know everything already, but you've learned more about yourself while gaining in strength and responsibility, and figuring out how you can improve more in the real world as you get older. In the movie *Guess Who's Coming to Dinner?*, Sidney Poitier says to his father, 'Dad, I love you but you think of yourself as a colored man. I think of myself as a man.' This quote describes me. I think of myself as a man, not an autistic man."

Less than a week after graduation, we watched him pass through airport security, alone, to travel solo across the country to hobnob with cousins. When he returned, he opened debit and credit card accounts, began college, and started his first paying job. The photo of him brandishing his first paycheck racked up the most "like" statuses of anything I ever posted on Facebook.

The process of guiding your child with autism to adulthood is fraught with sly subtleties. It's influenced by not just the deliberate actions you take, but also the actions you don't take, the actions you take without careful consideration, the things you say, the things you don't say, the perspectives you inhabit, the attitudes you project, knowingly or unintentionally. So before your child leaves childhood behind, there is one more thing this mother of a come-of-age child with autism wants you to know.

Your child or student will become a reflection of your perspective and the perspective of those who teach and guide him.

Perspective is an amalgam of attitude, intention, empathy, and information—the quality thereof, or the lack thereof. Whether deliberate or unconscious, the perspective you form about your child, his autism, his future, and the role you play in his life colors all you do and say, and creates the prism through which you present your child and yourself to the world.

A remarkable paraeducator named Nola Shirley guided Bryce through his first three years of school. Teachers called her Magic Nola because she engendered the kind of trust in children that gained her compliance and cooperation where others failed. She brushed off her so-called secret of success as "simple," describing it like this: "I never asked him to do anything I wasn't willing to do myself. Whatever 'it' was, we did it together."

Simple advice, maybe. But profound in its effect. I followed it religiously. I still do. More than once, it has booted me out of complacency, out of attitudes I hadn't recognized as smug, but were. It forced me to set the higher example, to stretch myself, emotionally, mentally, physically. Like any stretch, it's a strain at first, but with enough practice, you become limber, agile. You don't want to be any other way. Are you willing to do this—to ask nothing of your child that you can't or won't do yourself?

Throughout this book we've contemplated how perspective shapes our relationship with the child with autism. Now we are ready to face the mirror, shift our attention squarely to ourselves, whether parent, educator, family member, friend, or caregiver, and suggest that everything that applies to the child also applies to us. In what ways do the Ten Things about the child work in you?

- How do you define yourself, what words do you use, and what words make you cringe?
- What sensory experiences and sensations drive you batty, comfort you, distress or invigorate you?
- Do you distinguish between can't and won't in your own life?

- What's your thinking style? Can you appreciate how it dovetails or clashes with that of the child?
- Beyond your words, how do you communicate your wants and needs, your worldview?
- What do you "see" in your world, and is it literal or figurative? What's your primary learning mode, and how does it compare or contrast to the child's?
- Are you a can-do adult? Is your life mostly negative, positive, neutral, uneventful?
- What's your social quotient, and do you respect and accommodate those who differ?
- What challenges your ability to self-regulate? What drives you to meltdown (internally or externally)?
- Do you love yourself unconditionally enough to be able to, in turn, love a child that way?

The power of perspective-taking can reach its peak or can bottom out under the demands a child's autism places on an adult. I wish I understood why some parents and family members are able to rally to the charge autism puts before them, to embrace their child's autism as a catalyst and an opportunity for personal growth for all, while others stall out, turn away and grit out the years, existing but not living, waiting to pass some charmed milestone that will render the child a socially, emotionally, and cognitively accomplished adolescent or adult. Likewise, I'm perplexed as to why some professionals regard each child's unique faceting as a welcome engagement, while others don't seem to see past their aggregated years of repeated experiences to the individual child who doesn't fit the profile of any other. The mental agility that some parents and professionals seem to be able to achieve while others don't is a movement integral to the child's future development, cementing inside the parent, *I will do, can do, whatever it takes to help this child.* That perspective shift comes alive not in just how you view the child, but in how you view yourself, and how you handle the cards you've been dealt. One is indivisibly intertwined with the other, forevermore affecting the child and determining how he grows into adulthood.

"Your life is what your thoughts make of it," observed Marcus Aurelius. For the child with autism, we must extend that: your child's life is what your thoughts make of it. More than any treatment, diet, or therapy, the perspectives from which we view a child's autism have the greatest impact on whether he will learn to grow, thrive, and be a happy person. If you spontaneously added "in spite of his autism" after "happy person," it illustrates how ingrained a limiting perspective can be. It makes no difference if that restrictive thinking is conscious or subliminal; the result is the same.

Throughout Bryce's adolescence, he pushed across boundaries that to him represented risks worth taking. At twelve, he asked a girl to the movies. At thirteen, he travelled across the country with a school group. At fifteen, he rode public transportation all over town. At eighteen, he reported for jury duty. At each of these achievements, I would hear from at least one parent of a child with autism, "I can't imagine my child ever doing that!" And my fists would ball up between my knees in frustration and I would cry, "Why? Why can't you imagine it? If you can't imagine it, he may never live it."

Our children depend upon us to create in ourselves and in others a perspective that empowers rather than obstructs. Obstructive perspective can fester undetected, and often it is supported by the commonest tool in the shed: self-sabotaging language.

Words are inspiringly and insidiously influential. They linger on the job long after they leave our lips, keyboards, and pens. Steeped as we are in the world of autism, we sometimes lapse into its lingo, aloud and in our thoughts, without consciously asking ourselves if these buzz phrases or catch words fairly or fully describe our child, and making the perhaps unconscious assumption that when spoken, our listener will read between the lines and take our deeper meaning. We may not even see the chasm between our words and our meaning, and our listener has no reason to suspect there is one, let alone to step across it. And therein lies the danger.

From next-door neighbors to a panoply of professionals, from the friends we choose to the relatives and classmates we can't choose, everyone who interacts with a child with autism must heed the impact of their words. The words you choose to think of and describe the child and her autism underline your own attitude about her, the role you play in her autism, and about autism in general, whether as an organic thing or as an inert megalith. But larger than that, the belief-powered language with which you describe a child's autism sculpts what others believe about her and her potential. It frames their expectations, the attitude and manner with which they will interact with her, maybe even their willingness to interact with her. It influences how they will represent her to others.

The lingo of autism often rolls through our heads and off our tongues without our being aware of the condescension and scorn that underlay some of the commonly used terminology, labels, and characterizations of our children with autism. They tantrum, they obsess. They're finicky.

They suffer. Not only does a lifetime of listening to these messages impact a child's self-esteem and sense of worth, but our using these terms around others reinforces the slur and tacitly gives permission to perpetuate and spread it.

Giving up derogatory terminology and setting the better example for others begins with ditching the idea that carefully considered language is "just semantics." The interrelationships of words and phrases that create meaning in language are every bit as intricate as the interrelationships between people. Just as we have to tenderly care for and build these relationships with others, we have to also consciously build a frame of mind and a vocabulary that defines our child's autism accurately but respectfully and without denigration.

And just as we explored in Chapter Eight how social thinking must begin at its roots, so does healthy perspective building begin with exposing the attitude that underlies our words.

Tragedy

A few years ago, I spotted a short article in a neighborhood newspaper. A local mom of a five-year-old with autism and an experienced behavior therapist had launched an autism center offering consultative services for custom home programs, family support and training. *Oh, happy day,* I thought, until the next sentence put a pin in my balloon. A local business owner had jumped in to support this promising new venture by donating a portion of sales. "We wanted to help," he said. "Autism is a tragedy for families."

It goes without saying that the support, financial and emotional, of our local communities is deeply appreciated. But I cannot say this more strongly: Autism is a tragedy for families *only if they allow it to be. The greatest tragedy that can befall a child with autism is to be surrounded by adults who think it's a tragedy.*

Even during our darkest struggles with autism, I viewed it as a multi-dimensional gauntlet, an obstacle course, an alternative route. But never, ever a tragedy. If I had viewed it as such, it's unlikely I would have experienced the never-to-be-duplicated moment that unfolded when Bryce and I paid our first visit to his new, post-pediatric primary care doctor. She asked him if his autism affected his life. Not *how* does your autism affect your life, but *does* it? Bryce answered, with complete aplomb, that it didn't affect his life as much as it had as a child "because, you have to understand, in that regard I had the perfect mother."

No mom who is reading this will have to guess my reaction: bawling in front of a doctor I'd known less than ten minutes. ("Sometimes we get moments like this," she whispered to me.) I expected Bryce to backpedal a bit, maybe saying, oh c'mon Mom, you know what I mean. But no. He looked at me, then the doc and said, "What? It's true. She did everything she could for my autism, so it's much less of an issue now."

Tragedies by definition don't have happy endings. Great for Shakespeare, not for us. We get to choose, and we don't have to choose between heaven and earth, between attitude and altitude. We can have both. Perhaps you're already there. Perhaps your perspective is just the opposite of tragedy.

And therein lies a different sort of danger.

Perfect

I can be forgiven for swooning over Bryce's dubbing me a perfect mother, but anyone who's spent an hour as a parent knows that perfection is out of the question. At the opposite extreme of tragedy lies a perspective just as limiting. In its sincere but casual use, "perfect" may be just as dangerous as "normal" or "disabled." Perfect, by definition, means "flawless." No one is perfect, and that's an immutable fact. While some family members still confront autism with grief, denial, anger, and blame, an increasing number of parents tell me their child is "perfect just the way s/he is." They don't like references to autism as a disorder, "when in fact my child was born perfect." They believe "everything will be perfect if I just love this child." Online I found a "My Perfect Child" autism community and blog postings with titles such as "The Perfect Ten About Your Child with Autism."

To the child who thinks in concrete terms, interprets language literally, and experiences life's tribulations and triumphs as black-and-white, all-or-nothing propositions, "perfect" sets up a bar of expectation that fails on both ends, and in the middle. The standard of perfection is unattainable, so the child thinks, why even try? Or the standard becomes one of complacency: if I'm perfect, I don't have to try. Or, it creates a state of confusion and anxiety: Mom says I'm perfect, so why is everyone else always ragging on me?

Sending our kids the message that they're perfect doesn't serve them well in a world that constantly tells them otherwise. Far more useful is to imbue them with the understanding that in everyone, *everyone* are issues and aspects to improve upon, refine, discover, master. Every. Single. Person. Without. Exception. This is one of life's few absolute truths upon which your child can rest his full weight. Success as an adult, not flawlessness, must be the goal toward which we guide every child, because it's an aspiration both vital and attainable. "Perfect" no more exists and is no more worth striving for than "normal."

Excuse

Neither you nor your child had a choice about his autism, and autism may indeed be the reason for some of your child's behaviors and learning difficulties. But letting it become an excuse will handicap him more surely than autism itself. There's a difference between a reason and an excuse: reason explains the fact of a problem or situation, while an excuse attempts to justify, usually through denial or deception.

At graduation, Bryce received wonderful letters of encouragement from all his teachers. The one that most stood out to me came from his English teacher, who herself has ADD, dyslexia—and two master's degrees. She advised, "You are going to have to work harder, longer, and smarter than your friends in order to survive. Get over it now and start getting stuff done!"

A small Halloween incident at our house a few years ago brings this into focus. A princess-costumed trick-or-treater renounced our candy offering with, "I don't like Skittles!" And, sneering at the Tootsie Rolls, she whined, "What are those? I don't like them either."

The incident appalled me, but many of my Facebook readers weren't at all concerned, responding like this: The child might have been on the spectrum. We all know that spectrum kids have no filters. Yeah, my spectrum kid might have done the same. They call it like they see it. Laugh it off; it's her parent's problem, not yours.

This astonished me. It hadn't crossed my mind that the child might be on the spectrum because her behavior was rude, period. Being an outspoken, filterless, spectrum child may be a reason for such behavior, but it's no excuse. I related the incident to a group of professionals that included teachers, health workers, and clergy. In sharp contrast to the parent group, they found the girl's behavior not amusing or excusable, but alarming. They extrapolated the behavior, if uncurbed, down the developmental timeline. Imagine the impact of such behavior at birthday parties ... holidays ... as a houseguest ... as a member of a team or club ... in the workplace.

Most often when we raise an excuse, we do it deliberately and often with considerable forethought. Much more subtle and perhaps subliminal is the thought process that can lead us to evoke our child's autism as an excuse to forego teaching. In the most loving families and the most experienced teachers, we see examples of it at every stage of childhood. It happens when parents or teachers treat their child or student with autism as something other than a full member of the family or classroom, with developmentally appropriate responsibilities to others. It happens when we allow the child a sense of entitlement, rather than teaching from an early age the concept of earning, be it privileges or money. We see it when we defer teaching mundane but essential daily life skills either out of pity or out of impatience for the length of the teaching process ("she's so slow/doesn't do it right; it's easier and quicker to do it myself").

And we see a very sad story in the making if we use our child's autism as an excuse to avoid the harder conversations that come as adulthood approaches and the stakes get higher, conversations about things like sex and drinking, where one mistake can have devastating long-term consequences.

The irony of the reason-versus-excuse counterpoint is that a concrete-thinking child with autism learns responsibility-avoidant behavior from the people around him, when his own natural inclination would be toward fact. I saw this in Bryce throughout high school, when he learned to identify the cause of a less than optimal result without self-incrimination or denial, and use it as a stepping stone to a better result next time. Of a poor test result, he might say, "I didn't allow myself enough time to study." Or, "I didn't understand the assignment and I should have asked the teacher to explain further." For his parents and his teachers, ensuring his future as a self-sufficient adult was all the reason we needed to disavow and disallow excuses.

Words

The louder the conversation about autism becomes, among ourselves and across the media, the more aware we need be of the emotional quotient of the words we use to describe our children. Some examples of words that subtly undermine our kids:

Tantrum. Meltdown and tantrum are sometimes used interchange-ably to describe an out of control child, but such usage is incorrect. Think of the imagery created by each of these words. "Meltdown" conjures a fearsome and destructive event triggered when conditions rooted in physics or chemistry reach a tipping point. "Tantrum" conjures a petulant human. The source of a child's tantrum is frequently obvious; he didn't get the cookie or doesn't want to share the swing.

With time and instruction, most children's communication skills and self-awareness mature to where they can make their needs known without losing emotional control. In the child with autism, the source of the meltdown often baffles the adults around him, springing from unrecognized sensory or emotional overload, compounded by as-yet inadequate communication skills. He cannot "outgrow" the behavior without neutralizing the source.

Obsessive. Google "autism obsessive interest" and you'll get a million hits, many making stereotypical statements like "Children with Asperger's usually develop an *obsessive interest* in a single subject." While it's common for children with autism to develop a circumscribed interest in a single thing, many so-called typical adults behave the same way, whether their devotion is to sports, music, gaming, their jobs. When people get paid for their obsessive interest, we call them overachievers and acknowledge that they are "passionate" about what they do. When a person is sports-obsessed, we call them a fan or an aficionado. I know people who are obsessive about wine; they call themselves connoisseurs. What makes some interests obsessive (we frown . . .) and some passionate (we admire . . .)? Bryce started ninth grade not knowing a soul in his new high school. His first friendship there blossomed when he met a student who shared an interest in Thomas the Tank Engine (the original 1930s stories) that lingered past childhood. He and Bryce still go to train shows together. These shows are staged by—yep, adults who are "obsessive" about their model train layouts. Keen, avid, passionate interests can lead to the very things so many parents crave for their children with autism: social communities (clubs, teams, classes, conventions), friendships, and careers.

Picky. "Picky eater" is a derisive term many adults sling around to describe those whose food preferences are more selective than their own. Consider our initial reactions to the words "selective" and "picky." Selective = discerning. Picky = fussy. But everyone is selective about what they eat; the only variable is degree. I know a number of people who claim they'll eat anything. Press them on this and within a few sentences, they'll insert the caveat, well, anything except oysters, or beets, or coconut, or bologna, or okra. Many adults choose restrictive diets without falling subject to the arrogance of others designating them as picky. People who choose not to eat meat are vegetarians. Jews choose foods that are kosher; Muslims choose foods that are halal. People who disdain foods or ingredients they consider inferior call themselves gourmets. A disrespectful attitude about eating habits teaches a child, well, disrespectful name-calling and negative self-image. "Enjoys a few things" is a more accurate description that preserves the child's dignity while giving him a foundation to build upon, one bite at a time. I know whereof I speak. Bryce's limited palette continues to be one of the more challenging aspects of his autism. However, my job was to educate him on the building blocks of proper nutrition, and to teach him the skills needed to prepare foods he liked. If he chose a balanced diet based on repetition rather than variety, the key word was balance, not variety. With our instruction and encouragement, he did that from a young age.

Suffer. A short news story titled "Living with autism" appeared on the website of a Midwest newspaper. It described an eight-year-old girl who "lives her life like any other child her age," grappling with math, squabbling with her brother, playing with friends at the park despite "suffering from autism." The girl's mother "wouldn't trade her for the world," and said she's luckier than many, as her daughter "only suffers from a mild case of autism." (Mom's words, or the reporter's? We can't tell from the way the story is written.) Alongside the article ran a photo of a gorgeous, beaming mom and her lovely young girl, arms wrapped around her mother's neck in the kind of hug we all live for.

That was two "suffers" in an article of barely 300 words, an article that describes an affectionate, "happy, always smiling child" who lives a "largely normal life" (we'll ignore the word "normal" for now) and a mother who "loves being a parent." So is this girl suffering from autism, or does she suffer from thoughtless, clichéd language perpetuated in the twice-removed arena of the media? The author of the article may not have made a conscious choice to employ a lazy catch-phrase that actually contradicted the content of his piece. But he could have chucked the "suffering" and the "disorder" and wrote instead "... her daughter's autism is mild and she can attend public school and live a largely normal life ...."

It's important to celebrate children who live with autism rather than suffer from autism because many children truly do suffer from their autism. From physiological ills to debilitating sensory dysfunction to anxiety and hyperactivity to isolating social skills deficits—yes, many children with autism suffer. *But not permanently.* With education, therapy, patience, encouragement, and training, countless children with autism learn and adapt and overcome and thrive. That's all anyone can aspire to, autism or no. It starts with stamping out suffering—where it doesn't exist.

Semantics—that rubric of infinite angle and emotion, the bacchanal of words from which we choose to inform, entertain, comfort, castigate, exalt, lament, discourage, compel, empower. *We choose.* Without feelings of respect, what is there to distinguish men from beasts? asks Confucius. Any growth we hope to encourage in our children, and any consideration for them we hope to engender in others has to start from a position of respect and the language to fortify it.

In a sweet vignette I read many years ago, an American couple travelled to Capri where, in a tiny café perched on a towering cliff, they met a man who claimed to speak English. The couple understood not a syllable of the stream of words pouring out of the man as he led them to a balcony with a view of a steaming Mt. Vesuvius and the glittering Gulf of Naples. There, he gestured to the breathtaking grandeur and exclaimed, "Da panoram, she is so *very!*"

The diction and grammar may have been crude, but the man's perspective and intent were crystal clear. He wanted visitors to his beloved homeland to take in all the eye could see, looking up, down, sideways and behind, because the more they looked, the more they'd see, the more they'd marvel at what they'd discovered, the more they'd find to do and the more they'd want to stay and do more. Your child's autism is like that. It invites you to live in the perspective of a flexible thinker and seeker, curious, engaged, and always wondering, envisioning, and doing all you can to expand life's experiences, for the child, for the family, and then by example, for others not involved with autism. Only by widening your own perspective can you inspire the child to do the same, that he may see himself as more, so much more, than his autism, that he may embrace and live the conviction that the "panoram" life offers can be so *very.*

Bryce stood in the kitchen some months after graduation, chugging orange juice and loading slices of cheddar cheese onto sourdough bread. With the clarity that often comes with time and distance, he told me that he had spent his high school years trying to define himself. How would he fit into a world that viewed him as different, yet remain true to the vision of himself that he'd cultivated so carefully, and liked?

A fine line walked by many, I started to say. But I should have known that he had arrived there ahead of me. His smile, small but heart-melting, leaked quiet and comfortable self-confidence. He said:

"I knew I wasn't 'autistic' and I knew I wasn't 'normal,' whatever that is, so I chose something else. I chose to be optimistic. That's how I define myself."

Appendix

Questions for group discussion or self-reflection

More by Ellen Notbohm:
Book excerpt, *Ten Things Your Student with Autism Wishes You Knew*

Questions for discussion and self-reflection

Preface and It Begins . . .

- Throughout the book, the author notes she had to learn from her son to be able to teach him. Discuss this concept of circular learning as it applies to your child or student.

- The author alludes to people allowing autism to have "authority and power" in their lives. Do you agree or disagree with this concept?

- The author suggests reframing a child's troublesome characteristics or behaviors as positives. List three traits, habits, or behaviors of your own that others might find odd, quirky, or irritating. Explain how they benefit or fill a need for you. Then do the same for your child or student.

- Do you believe the author's statement that she is "having a good time on this trip"? Why or why not? Are you "having a good time on the trip"? Why or why not?

- The author details some of the thoughts that motivated her to be as strongly involved in her son's life as she was. What motivates you to advocate and work with your child, or to work with students with autism?

Chapter One

- In your experience, does hearing the term "autism" automatically bring up associations of limitations or "less than" among the general public? Among other parents of children with autism or Asperger's? Among educators and service providers? If so, do you view that as positive or negative, and why?

- Name three preconceived notions you or others associate with the word "autism."

- The author suggests, "...what you choose to believe about a child's autism may be the single biggest factor affecting his ultimate outcome." Do you agree or disagree, and why?

- The author takes a strong stance against "putting the adjective before the child." Discuss the different perceptions (your own and those that arise in others) associated with using "child with autism" versus "autistic child."

- How does your local media portray autism? Do you think it's an accurate portrayal? If not, what could you do to change it?

Chapter Two

- Why does the author suggest throughout the book that sensory issues be the first consideration and accommodation made for the child with autism or Asperger's?

- Identify three settings or environments where sensory overload might cause your child or student to melt down or otherwise react negatively (flee, shut down).

- What accommodations can you make to home or school environments to ease the child's hyper- and hyposensitivities?

- Do you resent, or are you reluctant to make sensory accommodations for the child? Why?

- Discuss the different ways auditory challenges (hyper- and hypo-) can affect the learning abilities of the child in a group setting.

Chapter Three

- In light of reading this chapter, describe specific instances in which your perception of your child or student's behavior has shifted from "won't" to "can't"?

- To what extent do you consider autism or Asperger's to be the source of your child's "can't" or "won't" behaviors? Discuss whether or not some may be attributable to the child's basic personality, inadequate teaching, or environmental factors instead.

- Do you follow a 4:1 praise-to-criticism ratio in your daily interactions with your child or student with autism or Asperger's? If not, discuss reasons and possible strategies for achieving a more positive praise-criticism quotient.

- In what ways might your own behavior toward your child or

student with autism or Asperger's be confusing, illogical, negative, or unsupportive?

- How does a parent or teacher determine whether a child with autism or Asperger's is being manipulative with behavior or is truly in need of assistance in understanding the situation at hand?

- What strategies have you developed to help yourself get through difficult moments so you can be a "can do" parent or teacher?

Chapter Four

- During group discussion or in your family setting, flag each usage of idiom, metaphor, slang, pun, inference, allusion, double entendre, or sarcasm. Rephrase in concrete language. For the next few days, keep track of your own usage of imprecise language. How does this awareness change the way you communicate with your child or student? How does it change his response to you?

- Brainstorm ways in which you might teach your child or student common idioms.

- Discuss ways you can demonstrate, in verbal and nonverbal ways, that you are listening and hearing what the child is trying to communicate.

- Create a short list of communication strategies you could post in the classroom or at home to help others be more effective communicators with your child or student.

Chapter Five

- Discuss the different perceptions of ability held of children with autism or Asperger's who are nonverbal versus those who are verbal.

- Debate this statement: language ability and IQ are directly related.

- Discuss the difference between talking and communicating.

- List five nonverbal communication behaviors that are frequently used during conversation. How many of these behaviors can your child or student demonstrate appropriately? Are these nonverbal forms of communication included on the child's IEP? If not, why?

Chapter Six

- Identify three visual supports in your own life (calendar, cookbook, map, watch, etc.). How effectively could you function without them?

- What types of visual supports are employed in your child or student's classroom? In the home? Other venues? What level of ongoing teaching is provided on how to use the visual support?

- Discuss how visual tools support and build a child's ability to perform tasks independently and interact socially.

- What is "level of representation" and how does it figure into visual support strategies? How does a child's level of representation change over time, and how will that affect visual strategies and tools? When is it appropriate to phase out visual supports?

- Do you feel the use of visual supports draws undesirable attention to the child with autism or Asperger's as having a disability? If so, what technology or other options might be used instead to provide the same level of visual support?

Chapter Seven

- Do you consider your child or student's autism to be a disability or a different ability? Discuss the difference between the two.

- Draw a vertical line down the middle of a piece of paper. Write your child or student's name at the top. Title the left column "can do" and the right column "can't do." Set a timer for five minutes and list things the child can do on the left side. Set the timer again and complete the right column. Did your ideas stop before the timer went off? Entertain reasons why. Use this exercise to consider how easy/difficult it was to complete one side versus the other and what that may demonstrate about your perspective toward the child.

- How could you channel your child or student's strengths into opportunities for learning, recreation, or socialization?

- Can you identify your child or student's primary learning style? Can you identify your own learning style? How does it complement or clash with your child's? What tools do you provide him to facilitate his learning?

- Discuss or reflect upon the more prevalent nay-sayer comments you've heard about what a child with autism or Asperger's will "never do." How many of these do you consider to be true about your own child or student?

Chapter Eight

- Discuss what it means to have "good social skills."

- Why is teaching social skills by rote practice not enough?

- To what extent do you assume children with autism or Asperger's will learn social skills by being around and watching other children? How does that assumption impact the way you teach social learning?

- Discuss how a focus on social skills rather than social thinking impacts a child's ability to function in a group setting.

- Identify several ways in which social skills differ
  - from culture to culture
  - from setting to setting (home, school, church, park, visiting others' homes)
  - from relationship to relationship (family member, classmate, teacher, stranger).

- Does the child's teaching program give as much attention to social functioning as it does to an academic subject? Discuss possible reasons why or why not.

- When you teach a social skill, to what extent do you include a discussion of why (and the extent to which) the skill is important to the child himself and to others, and how it makes others feel, react, and respond? If you do so infrequently, discuss possible reasons this may be so and how to turn that around.

Chapter Nine

- Have you tried to squelch a particular behavior in your child or student without identifying or addressing its source? What was the result?

- Describe an undesirable behavior of your own, past or present. What need did or does it fill? Have you tried to extinguish the behavior? What did you try? How well did it work? Relate this to your efforts to change an undesirable behavior in your child or student.

- What self-regulation skills can be taught to the child at preschool age? At elementary school age? At early adolescence? At later adolescence?

- How might physical or physiological factors trigger your child or student's inappropriate behavior? What steps could you take to determine this?

- How might emotional factors trigger your child or student's inappropriate behavior? What steps could you take to determine this?

- What household or classroom rules do you enforce regarding respectful treatment of each other? Are there different standards for adults and children? Why?

- How important is it to model the behaviors you want from your child or student?

Chapter Ten

- What does "unconditional love" mean to you?

- Are you able to love your child or student unconditionally? Do you believe it's necessary or desirable? Why or why not?

- Do you or did you once view your child's autism as a tragedy? Has your thinking changed over time? How? Why or why not?

- How do you demonstrate acceptance of differences within your immediate family?

- The author suggests that bitterness can prevent an adult from experiencing unconditional love. What aspects of your life do you hold bitterness toward? What can you do to release these feelings and move on?

- The author suggests there is no "end of the road" when dealing with a child's autism or Asperger's. How does that idea make you feel?

Triumph and Transition and Evolution

- The author offers ten things she wants her high school senior to know as he transitions to adulthood. The advice is not autism-specific. Do you think it should be?

- Do you disagree with any of the ten things?

- What would you add to the list?

- Do you believe your child or student will be capable of living independently as an adult? Why or why not?

- Many people and elements contributed to Bryce's successes throughout his school years. What elements, conditions, environments, and attitudes do you think were most influential? What elements, conditions, environments, and attitudes have contributed to the successes your child or student has experienced? What elements, conditions, environments, and attitudes have impeded your child or student?

- What would it take to remove some of those impediments? Think beyond what may seem "reasonable" or "realistic" or "doable."

- The author cites terminology commonly applied to autism that she feels unfairly undermines individuals with autism or Asperger's. Do you agree? What are some other examples of such language?

Follow-up questions

- Prior to reading this book, what expectations did you have for your child or student with autism? Did anything in the book change your expectations? How? What, if anything, reinforced your existing thoughts?

- Prior to reading this book, what beliefs did you hold about autism in general? Did anything in the book change your beliefs about autism? How? What, if anything, reinforced your existing thoughts?

- If you were to hand this book to a friend or colleague, which points would you most want to convey?

- Will your child or student's life be different as a result of you reading this book? Will yours?

Book excerpt

Ten Things Your Student with Autism Wishes You Knew

condensed from

Chapter Three
I think differently.
Teach me in a way that is meaningful to *me*.

© 2006 Ellen Notbohm

FUTURE HORIZONS INC.

My raised-on-ROM children don't know whether to be amused or aghast at how their parents grew up in an era without CDs, DVDs, cell phones or computers. My first computer predated Windows. Back in those frontier days, you either had an Apple MacIntosh or an IBM personal computer. The Macs and the PCs were the Hatfields and McCoys. They not only didn't talk to each other, they *couldn't* talk to each other. They didn't "think" alike. Your student with autism is like a Mac in a PC-dominated environment. He is hard-wired differently. Not incorrectly—differently.

For more than twenty years, Macs and PCs couldn't communicate with each other because their operating systems were not compatible. Such is life for the student with autism, whose basic operating system is different from those not on the autism spectrum. But your student can't wait twenty years for a solution to this incompatibility issue. We need to adapt our teaching to his operating system, now.

Learning to relate to the autism way of thinking challenges us because we have to be willing to step outside "normalcy." Collectively we are a social-driven society, all of us thinking and processing social and environmental inputs in a similar manner, our so-called typical thinking patterns naturally shared and naturally reinforced. To be able to truly understand a fundamentally dissimilar way of thinking requires you to suspend all you know and go somewhere you didn't even know existed.

This endeavor begins with a critical distinction. Your student's different architectural thought process has nothing to do with her abilities. We will never know the true extent of those abilities unless we establish communication via the architecture she has in place. We must disabuse ourselves forever of the idea that our student "could do it if he only tried harder." Also throw away the idea that all *you* have to do is "try harder." If we aren't trying through compatible channels, we can try until we cry and it won't ever matter.

This difference in architecture impacts the skills embodied in what we call critical thinking (classification, comparison, application), executive management (attention, planning, and memory functions) and social pragmatics (perspective-taking). These skills are missing from your students' hard-wiring. But *they can be taught.* Under patient and consistent instruction and coaching, children with autism can and do expand their social competence, improve executive functioning, and achieve a functional degree of flexibility in thinking and conversing.

How thinking is different in autism

At every turn in every day, we have the opportunity to help our student understand our patterns of communicating and relating, and teach those skills that are so elusive to the autism way of thinking. Keep in mind always that while the traits that follow may be characteristic, they will vary in degree from mild to profound.

The one—and only?—learning channel

Your student has one-channel wiring in a polyphonic world. He likely processes most information via the one learning intelligence that works best for him; in most students with autism, this will be visual or tactile; less commonly, auditory. He struggles to process multiple sensory modalities. For instance, he can listen, or engage in movement activities, or talk, but he may falter when required to process more than one of these tasks at a time. It can be especially difficult to listen and write at the same time.

Equally difficult is shifting back and forth between modalities (such as from visual to auditory and back again), and filtering out irrelevant sensory distractions.

A zillion parts in search of a whole

The typically-developing brain thinks general-to-specific. Your student with autism thinks specific-to-general. Consider how acute that difference is. For us, bits of data naturally, effortlessly sift into categories and subcategories. Did you have to consciously learn that banana, apple, grapes, and watermelon make up the category "fruit"? Bet you didn't; the category "fruit" just made sense.

Not so for your student with autism. His brain is like a cavernous warehouse filled with bits of unrelated information. As his teacher, you need to help him learn to organize, label, and cross-reference all that information, to teach him to think in categories. And your student's inability to form categories has an equally formidable cousin: the inability to generalize information. Every new experience exists in a vacuum. If you teach him to safely cross the intersection of Main and Smith Streets, that learning does not automatically apply to the intersection of 23rd Avenue and Johnson Drive. To his way of thinking, it's not the same.

Teach him to *categorize*. Start with simple, concrete categories like colors, clothes, or vehicles and build to categories that are less concrete, like function, proximity, or social categories like feelings. Explain why an object fits into one category or several, but not in others. Have him *compare and contrast* similarities and differences.

Teach him to *apply concepts*. Help him understand that categories can represent concepts, and that information can be inter-related, that you can take what you know about particular situations and people and objects, and use it in other settings and situations.

I need to see it to learn it

Many of your students with autism will be visual/spatial learners. They think in pictures rather than words. Your student might tell you:

> I need to see something to learn it, not just hear it. Words are frequently like steam to me; I know they are there but they evaporate before I have a chance to make sense of them. Information delivered in words comes and goes in an instant, and I don't have instant-processing skills. When information is presented to me visually, it can stay in front of me for as long as it takes to decode. Otherwise I live the constant frustration of knowing that I'm missing big blocks of information and expectation, and am helpless to do anything about it.

Over and over and over again

Children with autism are often characterized by their excessive selectivity and hyper-focus. Their extreme dependence on routine and sameness is a result of a thinking architecture that has difficulty processing change. Even small variations from expectation—taking a different route to school, having a substitute teacher, changing the student's desks around, create cognitive chaos that can domino-affect the entire course of the day.

Teach him to think *flexibly and cohesively.* With frequent, incremental opportunities for practice, he can learn to take life's little speed bumps without bottoming out. Where he is excessively selective and hyper-focused, teach him that

- there is more than one way to view a situation
- problems can have more than one solution
- ideas can be expressed and exchanged in different ways
- there is more than one "right" way to do most things

Teach him that knowing when to ask for help is as important as getting the answer right. Teach him to expect unpredictability as part of life, and that flexibility is not only necessary but can at times lead to fun and unanticipated enjoyment.

A one-sided coin

Your student with autism thinks in concrete, literal terms. Tell him to "shake a leg" and don't be surprised when he does just that. He's not being impudent; he's following your instruction. Metaphors, idioms, and figurative language are not part of his mindset.

In the classroom this can result in difficulty with problems that ask the student to summarize or synthesize, or pick out the theme or main point. It affects the manner in which he is able to retrieve information.

He might respond well to prompted retrieval, such as a multiple-choice or matching quiz. Difficulty skyrockets when he is faced with tasks entailing open-ended recall without the aid of prompting or cueing.

Everyone thinks like me—don't they?

Perspective-taking abilities are notoriously impaired in your student with autism. Until she is taught differently, she may believe that everyone in the world shares her same way of thinking, has her same thoughts about a person, event or situation, and shares her points of view. That inability to generalize applies here, too. Explaining a different point of view in one instance doesn't mean she understands that all people can have different ways of thinking in every different instance.

Perspective-taking is a social skill that involves knowing and understanding that the same words, events or objects may look, sound, or feel different to different people. It is considering the thoughts, feelings, attitudes, and beliefs of others before we speak or act. Many of the social/emotional gaps in your student stem from this impaired perspective-taking. He can't anticipate what others might say or do in different situations, nor understand that what one person does in a given situation, another person may never do! He may not even understand that other people have thoughts and emotions, and thus he may behave in ways that come across as uncaring or self-centered.

Without teaching these skills, your student may never experience the results and rewards of healthy perspective-taking ability detailed by Michelle Garcia Winner, speech/language pathologist, author, and veritable guru of teaching perspective-taking to individuals with autism:

- To interpret the needs and wants of others
- To offer empathetic responses
- To safely navigate around persons who may have ill intentions
- To interact with nuance so that others do not perceive you as too demanding or too straightforward
- To share in the interests of others even without sharing the same level of interest, purely because one can enjoy the relationship
- To engage in social critical thinking and personal problem-solving.

Teach your student with autism that people have different ways of thinking, feeling, and responding. That we initiate, share, and reciprocate actions with others, not merely attempt to control our own situation. That we take social cues from others without imitating their exact behaviors and words.

And never forget: *he does not understand* the reactions his behavior produces in others.

Start to see things differently

Teaching our children with autism will be an exercise in spitting into the wind if we are not willing to accept and respect that they think differently; then find effective ways to adapt our teaching accordingly. If we can't manage to be flexible in our own approach to teaching him, if we don't accept his basic mental functioning as valid, we can't expect him to respond with any degree of motivation or desire to connect to us or our world.

The sweet spot is a meeting place somewhere in the middle. We shift our thinking enough to be able to teach to his way of thinking in a meaningful way. Then he can learn to be more comfortable with our way of thinking, and to feel competent in our world. Little by little the familiarity between us grows. Macs now communicate with PCs, and the dawning of the 21st century brought about the first annual Hatfields and McCoys Reunion Festival. There's never been a better time to learn to take that different perspective, to "think differently." You and your student will both learn things you never knew you never knew.

Acknowledgments

My thanks go to everyone at Future Horizons who makes my books not only possible but successful, and none moreso than my editorial director nonpareil, Kelly Gilpin, who has the patience of ten saints and the tact of ten diplomats.

Veronica Zysk continues to be my muse, my soul sister, and so much more than the term "editor" can convey. Several books ago, I ran out of superlatives for what her work and solidarity mean to me, to my work, and ultimately, to my readers.

My mother Henny and my husband Mark are my North Stars.

Without my boys there would, of course, be no book. Connor and Bryce, against all statistical odds, I got you, the two greatest kids on the planet. You are the delightful, consummate embodiment of the words of one of my own favorite authors, Mark Twain: "My mother had a lot of trouble with me, but I think she rather enjoyed it!"

About the author

Award-winning author and mother of sons with ADHD and autism, Ellen Notbohm's books and articles on autism have informed and delighted millions in more than nineteen languages. Her work has won a Silver Medal in the Independent Publishers Book Awards, a ForeWord Book of Year Honorable Mention and two finalist designations, *Learning* magazine's Teacher's Choice Award, two iParenting Media awards, and an Eric Hoffer Book Award finalist designation. Her book *Ten Things Your Student with Autism Wishes You Knew* was named to onlinecolleges. net's list "The 20 Essential Books about Special Education." She is a contributor to numerous publications, classrooms, conferences, and websites worldwide.

A note from Ellen

Your feedback matters to me. The thoughts and theories, feelings and philosophies of my readers around the world formed the current that carried *Ten Things Every Child with Autism Wishes You Knew* along from a humble magazine article to the beloved book it became. Please contact me, either personally or in community.

emailme@ellennotbohm.com
www.ellennotbohm.com
Facebook: https://www.facebook.com/ellennotbohm
Twitter: EllenNotbohm
LinkedIn: Ellen Notbohm

Index